PURE KINGDOM

Studying the Historical Jesus

It was once fashionable to claim that Jesus could not be known as a figure of history and that even if he could be known in that way the result would not be of interest for faith. Both contentions have been laid to rest over the past twenty years.

Scholarship has seen archaeological discoveries, advances in the study of Jewish and Hellenistic literature, a renewed interest in the social milieu of Judaism and Christianity, and critical investigation of the systematic relationship between those two religions (and others in the ancient world). In the midst of these discussions — and many others — Jesus has appeared again and again as a person who can be understood historically and who must be assessed before we can give any complete explanation of the history of the period in which he lived. As he and his movement are better understood, the nature of the faith that they pioneered has been more clearly defined.

Of course, the Jesus who is under investigation cannot simply be equated with whatever the Gospels say of him. The Gospels, composed in Greek a generation after Jesus' death, reflect the faith of early Christians who came to believe in him. Their belief included reference to historical data, but also included the interpretation of Jesus as it had developed after his time.

The critical tasks of coming to grips with the development of the New Testament, the nature of primitive Christian faith, and the historical profile of Jesus are all interrelated. The purpose of this series is to explore key questions concerning Jesus in recent discussion. Each author has already made an important contribution to the study of Jesus and writes for the series on the basis of expertise in the area addressed by his or her particular volume.

Of the many studies of Jesus that are available today, some are suspect in their treatment of primary sources and some do not engage the secondary literature appropriately. **Studying the Historical Jesus** is a series of contributions that are no less sound for being creative. Jesus is a figure of history as well as the focus of Christian theology: discussion of him should be accessible, rigorous, and interesting.

BRUCE CHILTON
Bard College

CRAIG A. EVANS
Trinity Western University

Pure Kingdom

Jesus' Vision of God

Bruce Chilton

WILLIAM B. EERDMANS PUBLISHING COMPANY
GRAND RAPIDS, MICHIGAN

Published jointly 1996 in the United States of America by
Wm. B. Eerdmans Publishing Co.
255 Jefferson Ave. S.E., Grand Rapids, Michigan 49503
and in Great Britain by
Society for Promoting Christian Knowledge
Holy Trinity Church
Marylebone Road
London NW1 4DU

Printed in the United States of America

01 00 99 98 97 96   7 6 5 4 3 2 1

Library of Congress Cataloging-in-Publication Data

Chilton, Bruce.
Pure kingdom: Jesus' vision of God / Bruce Chilton.
p.   cm.
Includes bibliographical references and index.
ISBN 0-8028-4187-2 (pbk : alk. paper)
1. Jesus Christ — Teachings. 2. Kingdom of God — Biblical teaching.
3. God — Biblical teaching. 4. Bible. N.T. Gospels —
Criticism, interpretation, etc. 5. Bible. O.T. Psalms —
Criticism, interpretation, etc. I. Title.
BS2417.K5C49   1996
231.7′2 — dc20   96-2416
CIP

British Library Cataloguing-in-Publication Data

A catalogue record for this book is available from
the British Library

SPCK ISBN 0-281-05060-0

for

Jacob Neusner

Contents

Preface

The kingdom of God lies at the center of Jesus' message both as a fact and as a mystery. The fact, recognized by everyone from the first disciples of Jesus to the most skeptical of scholars, is that Jesus preached that the kingdom was at hand. The mystery, debated perennially by those inside and outside the Church, concerns what precisely Jesus meant when he spoke of God's kingdom.

The past hundred years have witnessed especially intense scholarly discussion concerning the kingdom of God. Albert Schweitzer, active at the beginning of the century, is still the most famous representative of the critical quest to understand the heart of Jesus' message. But the course of Schweitzer's career also typifies the unease provoked in the Church by the attempt to grapple with Jesus in historical terms.

When Schweitzer went to Africa, he did not go as a missionary. That had been his intent, but his views regarding Jesus were regarded as too radical by the sponsoring organization. He qualified as a physician and set up his famous hospital in Lambaréné, all because his critical stance was felt to be incompatible with Christian faith. Both faith and critical discourse suffered from Schweitzer's isolation from the community he wanted to serve.

The fundamentals of Schweitzer's stance will take up our attention in chapter 1, along with other influential theories. Before we enter into the world of theory, however, it will serve us well to reflect on the great divide that in practice has separated scholarly discussion of the kingdom from what people generally believe. Perhaps no topic better exemplifies a characteristic malaise of the twentieth century: the isolation of critical discourse from contemporary belief, and vice versa.

Since the time of Schweitzer, of course, the divide has widened. Scholarly discourse appears dense (at best) to most people who read the Gospels, and public discourse concerning the kingdom (whether in the Church or not) seems ill-informed to most scholars. The standard vocabulary of both kinds of discourse illustrates the problem. Scholars routinely debate whether the kingdom should be defined as "eschatological," a word that is easily defined, but without much meaning in the world in which most people live. Meanwhile, the idea that the kingdom of God refers to social improvement among people of goodwill is a commonplace in religious and political discussion, although scholars are virtually unanimous in finding that is *not* what the term refers to. So one side speaks only in technicalities, while the other speaks without reference to history.

Jesus spoke of the kingdom in a message of profound hope and fundamental challenge. Whatever one makes of what he said, whether one decides to believe or not, his perspective ought to be understandable. We can understand him from a historical point of view, whatever our stance in regard to faith: recent discussion of Jesus in history has established that beyond much doubt. But if it is true in general terms that we can know Jesus, then it must be possible to understand what he stood for. Just that, the kingdom of God, is conveyed to us powerfully within the Gospels. They invite us to share the power of that vision.

Jesus' vision of the kingdom is our concern here; scholars' theories and modern concerns will take up our attention only insofar as they might illuminate Jesus' position. That focus means that I will here speak directly of Jesus, but on the understanding that the Gospels reflect the stance of communities that came to faith in him. Where those with scholarly interests might like to pursue issues further, notes indicate some useful resources.

The Feast of Polycarp
1995

CHAPTER 1

The Elusive Kingdom

Beyond Albert Schweitzer

Schweitzer: The Truth of a Delusion

Over one hundred years ago, in the preface to what would prove to be an influential book, Johannes Weiss observed with pleasure that there had been a great deal of recent discussion about the kingdom of God.[1] The intervening years have seen that discussion boil into controversy, ease into fleeting consensus, erupt again into disagreement; we have seen everything but stable unanimity. Why has even a simple definition of the kingdom proved elusive?

One of the few points of agreement in scholarly discussion of the kingdom of God has been that we commonly say that the kingdom is "eschatological." Even then, there is disagreement over what "eschatological" means, and recently it has been claimed that Jesus' reference to the kingdom was "non-eschatological."[2] The course of modern discus-

---

1. The book was first published in 1892, and that first edition has been translated by H. Hiers and D. L. Holland as *Jesus' Proclamation of the Kingdom of God* (Philadelphia: Fortress, 1971).

2. Marcus J. Borg, *Conflict, Holiness & Politics in the Teachings of Jesus* (New York: Mellen, 1984); *Jesus, A New Vision: Spirit, Culture, and the Life of Discipleship* (San Francisco: Harper and Row, 1987); "A Temperate Case for a Non-Eschatological Jesus," *Forum* 2 (1986) 81-102. Borg's views are discussed below on pp. 16-22.

sion of the kingdom cannot be understood without a grasp of what the debate over eschatology involves.

The scholar most responsible for the conventional usage is Albert Schweitzer, whose entire career shows how difficult it can be to comprehend what Jesus said. Schweitzer's lifework, whether in or out of print, was to understand the significance of the kingdom as Jesus taught it. He certainly did not invent the idea of "eschatology." In 1894, while he was taking part in military training during the course of his studies, he was also reading Matthew's Gospel in Greek. Particularly as he considered the tenth chapter, with its reference to cataclysm on a cosmic scale, he conceived of Jesus' teaching as centering on the violent end of the world. Schweitzer had been influenced by nineteenth-century discussion of the literature of early Judaism. Documents that included calendars of the last things (the *eschata* in Greek, from which the term "eschatology" derives) especially aroused his interest.[3] It was logical — but also incisive — for Schweitzer to link his reading of Matthew with his theological curriculum on the one hand and the gathering storm between France and Germany[4] on the other.

What most of all struck scholars at the end of the last century was that in early Judaism "the kingdom of God" was used *neither* of an individual's life after death in heaven *nor* of a movement of social improvement on earth. Those had been dominant understandings of the kingdom, deeply embedded in the theology and preaching of the period. The brilliant and incontrovertible assertion of the basic significance of eschatology, first by Johannes Weiss and then by Schweitzer, changed all that.[5] They demonstrated that the kingdom of God in early Judaism and in Jesus' preaching involved God's final judgment of the world; the concept of the kingdom was part and parcel of anticipation of the last things.

---

3. For a detailed consideration, see B. Chilton, ed., *The Kingdom of God in the Teaching of Jesus* (Issues in Religion and Theology 5; London: SPCK/Philadelphia: Fortress, 1984); "The Kingdom of God in Recent Discussion," in *Studying the Historical Jesus: Evaluations of the State of Current Research*, Chilton and C. A. Evans (New Testament Tools and Studies 19; Leiden: Brill, 1994) 255-280.

4. That conflict was a particular source of grief to Schweitzer, who was born in Kaysersberg in the much disputed Alsace region. Even though he worked in Africa as a French citizen for the Missions Évangeliques, he and his wife were interred by the French government toward the end of the war. His wife never fully recovered her health. For discussion see M. Koskas, *Albert Schweitzer, ou le démon du bien* (Paris: Lattès, 1992) 139-145 and 147-164.

5. See the useful introductory material in *Jesus' Proclamation of the Kingdom* (n. 1 above).

Schweitzer's work was more famous than that of Weiss, but derivative in its content. It made "eschatology" and "apocalyptic" virtually synonymous: both words came to refer to cosmic catastrophe and final judgment *at an appointed time* in the future.[6] In the interest of clarity, "eschatology" should refer to an anticipation of divine judgment, while "apocalyptic" should refer to the calendar of the end, as is presented in a literary document that styles itself as an "apocalypse" (a revelation, the Revelation of John for example). In fact, however, usage of the two terms in scholarship has not been consistent. For Schweitzer, the way Jesus looked at the world, through the lens of eschatology, was simply untranslatable from our point of view.

Schweitzer's Jesus sent out the twelve to announce the kingdom's coming, by which he meant the dissolution of the world as he knew it. So fixed was Jesus' apocalyptic calendar that he expected that event before the mission of the twelve was done (see, above all, Matt. 10:23).[7] When the end did not come, he attempted to force his father's hand by offering himself for execution in Jerusalem. Jesus' thought was that God would not let the messiah die. Jesus on the cross was therefore an abject failure.

The stark picture that Schweitzer drew on the basis of what he called "consistent eschatology" has proven unappealing to those who see Jesus in sympathetic terms. When he first attempted to join the Missions Évangeliques in Paris in order to serve in Africa, Schweitzer was rejected. His eventual acceptance was conditional: he was to qualify fully in medicine, and to promise neither to preach nor to teach![8] Even those who have championed the use of eschatology in order to understand Jesus' teaching have not agreed with Schweitzer's elaboration of Jesus' plot to force God to bring on the kingdom.

The greatest opposition to Schweitzer has come from those who deny that eschatology tells us anything about Jesus' teaching. T. Francis Glasson, more than any other single scholar, has called attention to the degree of oversimplification involved in Schweitzer's position.[9]

6. Cf. Chilton, *The Kingdom of God*, 8, 9; A. Schweitzer, *The Quest of the Historical Jesus*, tr. W. Montgomery (London: Black, 1910, with many subsequent versions, from the German of *Von Reimarus zu Wrede*, which appeared in 1906).

7. The reference is, of course, to "the son of man" rather than to the kingdom. It is another weakness of Schweitzer's position that he conflates the two without justification.

8. See Koskas, 65-66, 77-80.

9. Cf. "Schweitzer's Influence: Blessing or Bane?" *Journal of Theological Studies* 28 (1977) 289-302, reprinted in Chilton, *The Kingdom of God*, 107-120.

Glasson's primary point "was to show the factual inaccuracy of Schweitzer's case";[10] although calendars of the last things are indeed available in apocalyptic literature, the phrase "kingdom of God" simply is not usually found in such a setting.

The reason eschatology has been so hotly disputed is that, as Schweitzer observed, it is not translatable into modern terms of reference. The prevailing fashion during the nineteenth century was (as it is even now, to a surprising extent) to see the kingdom in terms of the progress that might be made by people of goodwill. Sometimes the progressive interpretation was applied only to people in the Church, sometimes more generally. Both readings were explicitly damned as fabrications by Schweitzer. It was crucial in his opinion that we acknowledge that "we no longer extend the kingdom of God upon the world."[11]

In his repudiation of a social interpretation of the kingdom, Schweitzer was again joining ranks with Johannes Weiss, who had also written against such an interpretation (even as represented by his own father-in-law, Albrecht Ritschl) in 1892. But the repudiation was far from complete. Although they conceived of the kingdom *in Jesus' teaching* as the destruction of the present world in favor of a new one, both Weiss and Schweitzer reverted to a progressive, social interpretation *when it came to their own thinking*. Weiss openly embraced Ritschl's theology as a conscious transposition of Jesus' theology into a new key, moral rather than eschatological.[12] For Schweitzer, the underlying question was one of *will*. If one grasps, or rather is grasped by, Jesus' intensity in desiring the kingdom and serving others, then — despite Jesus' obvious error — one is following him as the Christ. The fellowship of Jesus is a matter of sharing in his spirit by doing his work.[13]

The issue of Jesus' ethical will is the link between Schweitzer's academic work and his service to others. He once wrote:

10. In a letter written to me in 1990 (dated 26 January). I am grateful to Professor Glasson for his permission to cite his letter and for his encouragement over the years.

11. Schweitzer wrote in just those terms (*Nicht mehr dehnen wir das Reich Gottes aus auf die Welt*) to a conference in Bern in 1947. His letter is included in a useful collection edited by R. Grabs, *Albert Schweitzer. Denken und Tat* (Hamburg: Meiner, 1954) 68.

12. See Weiss, *Die Idee des Reiches Gottes in der Theologie* (Giessen: Ricker, 1901).

13. Schweitzer maintained the theme consistently in his life and work. A skillful and succinct resumé is available in Schweitzer, *Glaube*, ed. R. Brüllmann (Bern/Stuttgart: Haupt, 1982) 3-5.

4

All the problems of religion finally go back to one: that I experience God in myself other than as I know him in the world. In the world he encounters me as paradoxical, awe-inspiring creativity; in me he reveals himself as ethical will. In the world he is impersonal power, in me he reveals himself as personality.[14]

Ethical will, the activity of changing the world around us, was for Schweitzer the only way to reconcile the God within and the God without. "The two are one," he said, "but how they are, I do not understand."[15] Engagement with the world, not intellectual reflection, was the only true theology, and from the age of thirty on, Schweitzer dedicated himself to a life of "pure service." Service and theology were for him not merely complementary: service was theological, just as true theology could only be practical.   Nailed it.

Schweitzer's popular fame came from his medical work in Lambaréné (Gabon), which earned him the Nobel Prize for peace in 1952. He consistently linked his activity to his conception of the kingdom. He felt himself accountable to God for those around him; for them his very existence should mean that the kingdom of God had come.[16] It was vitally important, in Schweitzer's conception, that we should recognize that our fellowship with Jesus was also fellowship with God.[17] For that reason he could say, in nearly Ritschlian terms, that

14. *Alle Probleme der Religion gehen zuletzt auf eines zurück: dass ich Gott in mir anders erlebt, als ich ihn in der Welt erkenne. In der Welt tritt er mir als rätselhafte, wunderbare Schöpferkraft entgegen; in mir offenbart er sich als ethischer Wille. In der Welt ist er unpersönliche Kraft, in mir offenbart er sich als persönlichkeit.* (See Grabs, 163; Schweitzer, *Glaube*, 20.) In 1899, Schweitzer's dissertation on Kant's philosophy of religion was published. The Kantian influence on him (as on Weiss, though in his case largely mediated by Ritschl) is evident. Kant's pure and practical reason are here put into an explicitly theological key.

15. *Glaube*, 10: *Beide sind eins; aber wie sie es sind, verstehe ich nicht.*

16. Cf. Schweitzer, *Glaube*, 12. The German is more majestic, but it does not translate well, word for word, into English:

> *Ich möchte, daß man es an uns spürte, das wir das Leben scher nehmen, und in jedem Augenblick unserem Herrn gegenüber uns verantwortlich fühlen für das, was unser Dasein für die Menschen, mit denen wir zusammen sind und was es für das Kommen des Reiches Gottes in unserer Umgebung bedeutet.*

17. Cf. *Glaube*, 7: *In der Gemeinschaft mit Christus verwirklicht sich die Gemeinschaft mit Gott, wie sie uns bestimmit ist.*

acceptance of Jesus' spirit amounted to the arrival of God's kingdom.[18]

The dualism of God within and God without was finally overcome in Schweitzer's conception. By serving others in accordance with Jesus' ethical will, one realized the "reverence for life" intended by God in the very act of creation. External creative power and internal personal revelation were united in service, and only in service. The kingdom of God was effected by our devotion to a teacher who had himself been mistaken about the kingdom.

Ethics and Eschatology

Weiss and Schweitzer clearly understood the distinction between historical exegesis and modern theology. Both men transferred the reference of the kingdom from eschatology to ethics on the basis of a factor not in the texts to hand. *Or was it there?* Both Weiss and Schweitzer in fact considered Jesus' call to discipleship and to love of one's neighbor, each instances of the ethical dimension of his message, to be abiding imperatives. Schweitzer in particular grounded his concept of "reverence for life," the guiding theme of his mature years, in the message of Jesus. The key to religious living generally, such reverence came to willed expression in the case of Jesus, so that our wills might answer his. If the teaching of the kingdom indeed involves social consequences for everyone who acts upon the kingdom as Jesus did, how can a social interpretation be denied *as an exegesis of Jesus' own message?*

In response to the eschatological reading of Jesus that Weiss and Schweitzer pioneered, there have been a series of attempts to allow for the social dimension of Jesus' message. Sometimes, social constructions have been consciously and deliberately developed against an eschatological reading; sometimes, they are consistent with eschatology.

There have been efforts to portray the kingdom in Jesus' preaching as the Church, understood as the community of those who follow Jesus. Those who explore that possibility — notably Francis Glasson and Jean Carmignac — have had in mind, not a hierarchical conception, but the

18. Cf. *Glaube*, 4: *Wir begreifen, daß das Kommen des Reiches herbeigeführt wird, daß Jesu Geist in unsern Herzen zur Macht kommt und durch uns in der Welt.*

fellowship that develops around loyalty to Jesus. Adherence to the message of Jesus creates the sphere of a kingdom into which we might enter.[19] Of course, the principal difficulty with that definition of the kingdom is that the New Testament uses a distinct vocabulary for the Church, the *ekklesia* of those called by Jesus. The fellowship presently enjoyed, for all its rich dimensions, seems unlike the triumphant and ultimate kingdom that — within that fellowship — people pray will come.

Church and kingdom, however, are held to be related in most accounts of the theology of the New Testament. Even Weiss and Schweitzer — despite their own eschatological conceptions of the kingdom — both referred to fellowship with Jesus as of central importance. For Weiss, the morality of the kingdom was to be worked out socially; for Schweitzer, a serving community was where the truth of Jesus' delusion might be realized. There has been much more agreement between eschatologists and anti-eschatologists than their rhetoric might suggest! Weiss and Schweitzer believed that Jesus' eschatology expressed a central truth: that the realization of the kingdom did not depend on human efforts alone.[20] The conviction that the center of the kingdom is divine, not social, is shared by Glasson and Carmignac with Weiss and Schweitzer.

Eschatologists and anti-eschatologists largely agree that fellowship with Jesus is involved with the realization of the kingdom of God. Their essential difference is that eschatologists hold that Jesus himself anticipated a purely future regime, while anti-eschatologists maintain that Jesus' purpose was to call people into the kingdom of his fellowship. The term "realized eschatology" was coined by C. H. Dodd as a way of arguing that Jesus taught and told parables in order to assert his own identity as the messiah. Jesus' eschatology was "realized" in the sense that he held that his hearers could personally and fully encounter God and God's promises in his own person.[21]

Discussion since the time of Dodd has acknowledged that the parables, and Jesus' teaching generally, portray the kingdom of God in

19. See Glasson, "Schweitzer's Influence: Blessing or Bane?"; J. Carmignac, *Le Mirage de l'Eschatologie. Royauté, Règne et Royaume de Dieu . . . sans Eschatologie* (Paris: Letouzey et Ané, 1979).

20. See Schweitzer, *Glaube*, 7, and the second edition of Weiss's *Die Predigt Jesu vom Reiche Gottes* (Göttingen: Vandenhoeck und Ruprecht, 1900) 69.

21. See above all Dodd's *The Parables of the Kingdom* (London: Nisbet, 1935).

dynamic terms, as of immediate consequence in the present. But almost no critical scholar has agreed that Jesus spoke simply of the present, and none would go along with the contention that the kingdom of God was a cipher Jesus used to speak of himself. Rather, the judgment of Rudolf Otto, Dodd's contemporary, has been confirmed time and again: in Jesus' own conception, he did not bring the kingdom; it was rather the kingdom that swept him along in its wake.[22]

Whether the kingdom is viewed as the Church or as a cipher for Jesus' identity as the messiah, the alternatives to an eschatological reading — as exegeses of Jesus' message — have a single failing in common. They both transfer the kingdom's center of gravity from God himself to Christ, whether Christ as the founder of the Church or Christ as the incarnate messiah.[23] To be sure, the New Testament itself reflects such a transfer, as primitive Christianity developed more and more into a religion separate from Judaism and centered on Christ as divine. The stark character of that development is measurable by the phrase "kingdom of Christ," used interchangeably with "kingdom of God," but only in what are among the latest documents in the canon.

The earliest such usage appears in Col. 1:13, one of the letters attributed to Paul but emanating from the circle of Timothy (ca. 90 CE). The putative authors — Paul and Timothy together (1:1, 2) — give thanks to the father for making believers worthy "of a share of the portion of saints in the light, who delivered us from the authority of the darkness and transferred us into the kingdom of the son of his love . . ." (1:12, 13). The continuity with Pauline emphases is obvious here, as is the statement from approximately five years later in Ephesians 5:5, where the putative Paul speaks of those who do not have "an inheritance in the kingdom of Christ and of God." For usages during the same general period, see Rev. 11:15; 12:10 (cf. 1:9) and 2 Pet. 1:11. The turn of phrase seems to have influenced the Gospel according to John, as well, when Jesus refers there to "my kingdom" (18:36).

A christological reading of the kingdom, in which the central focus

---

22. See Chilton, *The Kingdom of God*, 31, in the extract entitled "The Kingdom of God Expels the Kingdom of Satan." (The extract, on pp. 27-35, is from Otto, *The Kingdom of God and the Son of Man* [London: Lutterworth/Boston: Starking, 1938] 97-107.)

23. Cf. Bruce Chilton and J. I. H. McDonald, *Jesus and the Ethics of the Kingdom* (London: SPCK [in the series Biblical Foundations in Theology]/Grand Rapids: Eerdmans, 1987) 24-29.

is Jesus rather than God, is certainly defensible on theological grounds. The transfer of meaning involved — in the light of faith in the resurrection — is arguably more straightforward than in Schweitzer's appeal to the abstract notion of "reverence for life." But for our immediate purpose the operative point is that a christological reading of the kingdom involves a transfer of meaning; it was not Jesus' own reading of the kingdom, although it developed within the movement that bore his message.

The challenge to exegetes since the time of Schweitzer has been to allow for the social dimension of Jesus' thought without reverting to a reduction of the kingdom to one christology or another. At the same time, in order to allow for the social dimension, the rigidly apocalyptic definition of the kingdom as a regime simply to come at an appointed time in the future also needs to be superseded.

Christian thought, as well as scholarly discussion, has been in some confusion ever since Weiss and Schweitzer made their point. As we have seen, some scholars attempt to deny that Jesus' teaching was eschatological, although it is difficult to see how such promises as the feast with Abraham, Isaac, and Jacob (Matt. 8:11; Luke 13:28-29) exclude reference to a future definitively changed by God. On the other hand, awareness that Jesus referred to the future has caused some scholars to fixate on the issue of eschatology, as if Jesus' whole purpose were to provide an eschatological calendar (in the manner of apocalyptic literature). A kind of middle ground has been staked out by those who accept that Jesus' thought was indeed eschatological, but then try find a way around the difficulty that the world has continued on its less than cheerful way for some two millennia since it was supposed to be about to end. What sort of messiah can have been so mistaken? Scholars of the middle ground tend to argue that Jesus spoke of the end of things in order to dramatize his own claim to authority.[24]

None of the three approaches is entirely satisfactory. To deny the eschatology of Jesus is simply to eliminate from consideration a substantial element of what the New Testament says he taught. What is inconvenient for modern purposes should not be wished away from ancient sources. But to fixate on Jesus' eschatology makes him appear to be an apocalyptist in the manner of the book of Daniel, although

---

24. See G. R. Beasley-Murray, *Jesus and the Kingdom of God* (Grand Rapids: Eerdmans, 1986).

none of the Gospels can be called an apocalyptic work. Moreover, if Jesus preached a *single* calendar of the last things, it is difficult to explain the variety of apocalyptic expectations in the movement that he founded. Finally, to argue that his eschatology was a cipher for his own authority ignores the emphasis on the kingdom itself, rather than on his personal identity, in Jesus' preaching. The argument also leaves us with an anomaly: a conception of time that proves faulty is a curious advertisement for the authority of Jesus' teaching.

Once the challenge of eschatology has been appreciated, it is easy to understand why much Christian thought has been in a retreat from its own Scriptures for most of the twentieth century. "Liberals" have attempted to replace the kingdom with a social gospel, rooted in hopes for progress in the world as a natural and human system. "Conservatives" have attempted to replace the message of the kingdom with the insistence that the messenger himself is divine. Scholarly discussion of the kingdom in Jesus' preaching, meanwhile, has often been reduced to an unproductive debate between those who characterize it as eschatological and those who refuse to do so.

What has not been sufficiently recognized is that the kingdom of God was deeply embedded in the language of early Judaism as a means of expressing *God's activity in the world.* It misses the point to consider only what is possible within the world (the "liberal" perspective) or only the divine source of the kingdom's influence (the "conservative" perspective). To say that God is active in the world implies that the world as we know it is changing. To speak of the kingdom *denies* the truism that nothing changes in this world *and* the truism that God is best known as an immutable power beyond our realm. The point of speaking of God's kingdom is that God makes his realm ours.

Beginning some twenty years ago, a new alternative to an apocalyptic interpretation (unlike Dodd's and Glasson's) began to emerge, and today it is represented in several quarters. Perhaps the new development is best traced from the late work of Norman Perrin, though (as shall emerge shortly) it represents less the contribution of any single scholar than a common recognition among experts in the field that an apocalyptic reading of Jesus is too limited.

In *Jesus and the Language of the Kingdom*[25] Perrin drew on the

25. (Philadelphia: Fortress/London: SCM, 1976).

perspectives of Amos Wilder and Paul Ricoeur in order to revise the apocalyptic interpretation of Jesus, which he himself had earlier defended.[26] According to Perrin, reference to the kingdom invoked the myth of God as king, of his activity in creation and in the history of Israel. It functioned for Jesus neither as a sign that points only to one referent nor as a concept within a theological system, but as a symbol that conveys a reality without exhausting it.[27] If so, he reasoned, attempting to pin the kingdom down to a single temporal moment might be a misleading exercise as well as an impossible task.

During the same period in which Perrin engaged Jesus' reference to the kingdom from a literary perspective, I was conducting research at Cambridge (at first, under the supervision of C. F. D. Moule, but principally under Ernst Bammel). My own work, exegetical rather than literary, was submitted to the examiners in the same year in which *Jesus and the Language of the Kingdom* appeared and was published three years later.[28] Its argument related the usage of Jesus to that of the Targumim, the Aramaic paraphrases of the Hebrew Bible commonly used in synagogues.

Especially in the Targum of Isaiah, the language of the kingdom is employed to render passages that in the Hebrew original speak of God intervening actively on behalf of his people. When that personal intervention is spoken of, the Targum (as a paraphrase more than a translation) refers to the revelation of "the kingdom of God" (or "the kingdom of the LORD"). The emphasis is on the dynamic, personal presence of God — not on the nature of God in itself, but on his saving, normally future activity. The future-oriented, eschatological aspect of the kingdom is therefore to be acknowledged, in my view, but it stems from Jesus' view of God, not from a particular (apocalyptic) expectation

---

26. Cf. not only *The Kingdom of God in the Teaching of Jesus* (Philadelphia: Westminster/London: SCM, 1963) but also *Rediscovering the Teaching of Jesus* (New York: Harper and Row/London: SCM, 1967).

27. Cf. Chilton, *The Kingdom of God*, 19-21, and the excerpt from Perrin's book, pp. 92-106 = *Jesus and the Language of the Kingdom*, 16-32, 127-131, 197-199.

28. *God in Strength: Jesus' Announcement of the Kingdom* (Studien zum Neuen Testament und seiner Umwelt 1; Freistadt: Plöchl, 1979), reprinted in the Biblical Seminar series (Sheffield: JSOT, 1987). See also "Regnum Dei Deus Est," *Scottish Journal of Theology* 31 (1978) 261-270; *Targumic Approaches to the Gospels: Essays in the Mutual Definition of Judaism and Christianity* (Studies in Judaism; Lanham/London: University Press of America, 1986) 99-107. Perrin and I began a mutually appreciative — but all too brief — correspondence just before his death.

for the future.[29] That perspective has been confirmed by Jacques Schlosser in his characterization of Jesus as emphasizing the dynamic transcendence involved in the kingdom.[30] "The kingdom of God" fundamentally *is* God, as he manifests himself for his people.

The temporal aspect of Schlosser's argument (and mine), the claim that Jesus understood God — as the kingdom — to be *in the process of disclosing himself,* may be said to correspond to inaugurated or self-realizing eschatology.[31] This position is increasingly asserted as if it were a matter of course.[32] The Judaic language of the kingdom referred to God's own activity; the fundamental conception of God in himself was not submerged within a messianic emphasis in Jesus' preaching.

Jesus' preaching concerning the kingdom appears to have been a conscious *performance* of fresh meaning, a distinctive vision of the kingdom of God that also invited Jesus' hearers to the sort of activity he believed was consistent with that vision.[33] Those two aspects of the

29. For further discussion see Chilton, *The Kingdom of God,* 22-24. It should be noted that, since my earliest work, my dating of the Targum of Isaiah and of the prophetic Targumim in general has become a matter of consensus; cf. *The Glory of Israel: The Theology and Provenience of the Isaiah Targum* (Journal for the Study of the Old Testament, Supplement 23; Sheffield: JSOT, 1982); *The Isaiah Targum: Introduction, Translation, Apparatus, and Notes* (The Aramaic Bible 11; Wilmington: Glazier/Edinburgh: Clark, 1987). The model I developed for the Targum of Isaiah is applied in D. J. Harrington and A. J. Saldarini, *Targum Jonathan of the Former Prophets* (The Aramaic Bible 10; Wilmington: Glazier/Edinburgh: Clark, 1987); Robert Hayward, *The Targum of Jeremiah* (The Aramaic Bible 12; Wilmington: Glazier/Edinburgh: Clark, 1987); S. H. Levey, *The Targum of Ezekiel* (The Aramaic Bible 13; Wilmington: Glazier/Edinburgh: Clark, 1987); Kevin J. Cathcart and Robert P. Gordon, *The Targum of the Minor Prophets* (The Aramaic Bible 14; Wilmington: Glazier/Edinburgh: Clark, 1989).

30. Cf. Schlosser, *Le règne de Dieu dans les dits de Jésus* (Études Bibliques; Paris: Gabalda, 1980).

31. The phrase is a conscious refinement of Dodd's language, which was developed by Joachim Jeremias (see Jeremias, *The Parables of Jesus,* tr. S. H. Hooke [London: SCM, 1972]). The refinement was then cautiously accepted by Dodd himself; see the discussion by C. F. D. Moule in a later edition of Dodd's *The Parables of Jesus* (London: Collins, 1961) 5-9.

32. Cf. J. H. Charlesworth, "The Historical Jesus in Light of Writings Contemporaneous with Him," *Aufstieg und Niedergang der römischen Welt* II.25.1, ed. W. Haase (Berlin: de Gruyter, 1982) 451-476, here 469.

33. See Chilton and J. I. H. McDonald, *Jesus and the Ethics of the Kingdom* (London: SPCK, 1987 and Grand Rapids: Eerdmans, 1988) 16-17, 19-20, 24, 29-31, 35-37, 49, 52, 59, 61-63, 65, 67, 70-71, 74, 80, 95-96, 99-100, 106, 111-114, 117-121, 123-125, 128-131. The definition of performance as the articulation of motifs in order to convey

kingdom — vision and invitation — are evident in a saying from the source called "Q" (Matt. 8:11; Luke 13:28, 29):[34]

> Many will come from east and west
> and recline in feasting
> with Abraham and Isaac and Jacob. . . .

There can be no doubt of the emphasis on a future consummation in the saying, involving a particular (but unnamed) place, the actions and material of festivity (including the luxurious custom of reclining, not sitting, at a banquet), and the incorporation of the many who will rejoice in the company of the patriarchs.

Jesus' use of the imagery of feasting to refer to the kingdom, a characteristic of his message, is resonant both with early Judaic language of the kingdom and with his own ministry. The picture of God offering a feast on Mount Zion "for all peoples," where death itself is swallowed up, becomes an influential image from Isa. 25:6-8 on. Notably, the Targum of Isaiah refers to the divine disclosure on Mount Zion as "the kingdom of the LORD of hosts" (24:23); that is, the Targum extends the reference to God's rule in the Hebrew text of Isaiah to a *direct reference* to the kingdom of God. As a result of such reference, the feast on Mount Zion had its place as part of the anticipation of divine judgment in the time of Jesus.[35] Sayings such as the one cited above from "Q" invoke that imagery, and Jesus' practice of fellowship at meals with his disciples and many others amounted to a claim that the ultimate festivity of the kingdom had already begun.

The dynamic of God including all his people is not without its dark side, whether in Isaiah and or in Jesus' preaching. The Isaianic feast

---

meaning (p. 113) is the basis of my later distinctions between the meaning that Jesus performed, its transformation in cycles of tradition, and the construals of those earlier meanings within the Synoptic Gospels, *Thomas*, and John; cf. Chilton, *Profiles of a Rabbi: Synoptic Opportunities in Reading About Jesus* (Brown Judaic Studies 177; Atlanta: Scholars, 1989).

34. For a detailed analysis of the saying, see Chilton, *God in Strength*, 179-201. The significant differences between Matthew and Luke here show that "Q" was not the stable source some scholars claim that it was.

35. See the discussion in Chilton, *A Galilean Rabbi and His Bible: Jesus' Use of the Interpreted Scripture of His Time* (Wilmington: Glazier, 1984), also published with the subtitle *Jesus' Own Interpretation of Isaiah* (London: SPCK, 1984), 57-63.

on Mount Zion is to be accompanied by the destruction of Moab, the military enemies of Israel (25:10-12);[36] in Jesus' saying, the feast with the patriarchs includes the threat of exclusion for those whose pride has caused them to ignore Jesus' invitation (Matt. 8:12; Luke 13:28). The ethics of the imagery, which at first may seem to involve little more than an ethos of festivity, turn out to imply the dimension of judgment, as is natural in an eschatological expectation of the kingdom. The kingdom of God in the saying from "Q" is a feast for the future whose invitation is issued now by Jesus, so that response to the invitation is implicitly a condition of entry.

The image of a feast in Matt. 8:11, 12; Luke 13:28, 29 is developed along narrative lines in what is commonly known as the parable of the wedding feast, after the version in Matt. 22:1-10 (compare Luke 14:16-24). In the parable Jesus engages in the rabbinic method of using narrative to recommend how we should behave: the point of the parable is the ethical performance it calls for.[37] The feast is prepared, but invitations must be *accepted* in order to be effective, and God is ready to drag outsiders in rather than permit his festivity to go unattended. The parable is an interesting development of the festal imagery we have just considered: Who would conceive of the Isaianic feast being passed up by those invited? The Jesus of this tradition, however, conceives of the kingdom as sufficiently elusive to occasion a willful ignorance of it. The parable's narrative, that is to say, conveys the kingdom within a fresh perspective. The narrative is designed as performance, to speak in images of what the kingdom means for us, so that we might perform that meaning in a fresh activity.

The performance of meaning effected by the parable is not entirely a matter of reference to the imaginary world of the story that is told. Precisely because the parable concerns *God's* activity as king, it makes a claim within the experience of anyone who knows what a king is. God, the parable claims, has been brought to act sovereignly but surprisingly. His present offer is out of the ordinary. The extraordinarily bad, even violent, behavior of those who should have been guests provides the impetus for a radical expansion in scope of an increasingly insistent invitation: leave your cares (however legitimate) and join the feast; take

---

36. In the Targum "Moab" is used as a symbol for Rome, Israel's oppressor, and the reference is distributed through the chapter; see Chilton, *The Isaiah Targum*, 47-51.
37. See Chilton and McDonald, *Jesus and the Ethics of the Kingdom*, 31-37.

the opportunity of an invitation you could never have anticipated. The parabolic motif of the meal portrays divine action as begun, but not as perfected. The king's actions point toward the future as the locus of the kingdom's ultimate disclosure. Similarly, the ethical theme of the parable frames and encourages a wary, clever — even opportunistic — response to the disclosure that is under way, but not complete.

Although the kingdom of God is a theme that Jesus derived from the biblical tradition (in Targumic form), it obviously acquired a life of its own within his teaching. He did not limit his references to passages of Scripture with which the theme was associated. He did not even require a scriptural occasion in order to invoke the idea. He thought it could be known by means of his narrative parables, as well as within the world of Scripture. There is ample precedent among the rabbis for the notion that a narrative parable might disclose the way in which God is or will be king;[38] Jesus' distinctiveness lies in the way in which the theme of the kingdom is *consistently* at the focus of his concern.

The parables of growth are unusual in literary terms, since there do not seem to be precise analogies in the Rabbinic literature. They underscore the extent to which Jesus held that the kingdom was a matter of experience, something one might participate in by observation. Acuity in observation is demanded, because growth is not something Jesus takes for granted. Watchfulness is the condition apart from which growth cannot be enjoyed. In the parable of the man, the seed, and the earth, it is stressed that the farmer has no idea how the crop is produced, but that he wields his sickle at the right time nonetheless (Mark 4:26-29). Mustard seed becomes a "tree" (so Matt. 13:31-32 and Luke 13:18-19) or makes "big branches" (Mark 4:30-32) without an interval of time being indicated; the point is beginning and result rather than process.[39] These parables are told as a lens of the kingdom, so that the hearer might see how the kingdom of God reveals itself.

Growth as understood by Jesus has the same dimensions as the kingdom. It is aimed at the future and intervenes as miracle on the way to spreading itself abroad; it demands specific behavior and takes place only on prepared ground; its natural extension leads to greater and greater inclusion. A bivalent understanding of "performance," under which the

38. See again Chilton and McDonald, 31-37.

39. The hyperbolic comparison of start and finish is also evident in the parable of the leaven (Matt. 13:33 and Luke 13:20-21).

kingdom's meaning involves both eschatological vision and ethical engagement, allows free movement between indicative and imperative aspects of the kingdom, a movement that has troubled interpreters.

The emphasis throughout is on the divine eschatological action on which ethical response is predicated, so that the fundamental character of performance is transcendent, as Schlosser suggests. Jesus' preaching of the kingdom is in the first place an announcement of God's dynamic rule. Human response, which might generally be described under the category of repentance, is performed *as response,* not initiating cause.

Beyond Eschatology: Recent Discussion in North America

The fact that the kingdom is normally a challenge of the future removes the possibility of understanding it within the terms of reference of the present alone. The kingdom is *immanent* insofar as God's rule impinges on and elicits a response from those who live in the present, but the kingdom is not merely a matter of what people experience. At the same time, the kingdom cannot be reduced to human expectations of the future any more than it can be reduced to human experience in the present. The temporal ambivalence of the kingdom in Jesus' preaching, its presentation as both present and to come, attests its transcendent character.

In North American discussion an attempt has been made to renew Dodd's challenge of Schweitzer's eschatology, but in an innovative way. Instead of arguing that Jesus' reference to the kingdom advertised his messianic identity, several contributors — Marcus Borg being foremost among them — have maintained that Jesus spoke of the kingdom in order to refer to his own mystical or spiritual experience.[40] The key to the new

---

40. Borg, *Conflict, Holiness & Politics,* 261. Borg has offered a more popularly accessible account of his views in *Jesus, A New Vision: Spirit, Culture, and the Life of Discipleship* (San Francisco: Harper and Row, 1987). Symbolist and anti-eschatological readings are developed elsewhere in literary keys (cf. J. Breech, *The Silence of Jesus: The Voice of the Historical Man* [Philadelphia: Fortress/Toronto: Doubleday Canada, 1983]) and in psychological keys (cf. J. A. Sanford, *The Kingdom Within: The Inner Meaning of Jesus' Sayings* [San Francisco: Harper and Row, 1987]). Although such treatments are not sufficiently exegetical to merit consideration here, they suggest the extent to which an exclusively symbolist reading of Jesus comports with contemporary cultural tendencies. Cf. Borg, "A Temperate Case." Borg's position in print might be said to have been

approach is that the kingdom is said to "symbolize" Jesus' experience. In other words, it is not only that the phrase "kingdom of God" is redolent of symbolic meaning: Borg's point is that Jesus was a conscious symbolist who used the language of the future when he meant something else. In Jesus' understanding "the mystical perception of both self and world is *sub specie aeternitatis,* a vantage point beyond time from which ordinary consciousness and experience seem like a state of estrangement."[41] Later, Borg would conflate his picture of "mystical perception" with the "primordial tradition" that Huston Smith has posited as the common denominator of the experience of shamans in primitive cultures.[42]

Borg's analysis of the difference between his position and my own is precise and accurate:

> As I see it, this understanding is very consistent with Bruce Chilton's important recent works on the kingdom of God. . . . Though he does not make the connection to the primordial tradition, he concludes that Jesus' public announcement of the kingdom refers primarily to "God acting in strength," i.e., to "God's disclosure of himself," and secondarily to the human response to that disclosure.[43]

Exegetically, Borg has frequently accepted my readings, but at key points he must dissolve eschatological meanings that even he acknowledges are operative in texts with an appeal to his controlling notion of "the primordial tradition."

My reading of a saying already mentioned — Matt. 8:11, 12/Luke 13:28, 29 — is thoroughly eschatological, and that is part of my analysis of Jesus' public announcement that Borg does *not* cite.[44] Instead, he employs faulty logic in order to cut eschatology out of the text:

---

anticipated in B. B. Scott, *Jesus, Symbol-Maker for the Kingdom* (Philadelphia: Fortress, 1981), though the dissertation of which Borg's book is an extensive revision was submitted in 1972.

41. *Conflict, Holiness & Politics,* p. 238. Borg's Latin has been altered.

42. Cf. Borg, "A Temperate Case," 92, 93, citing Smith, *Forgotten Truth: The Primordial Tradition* (New York: Harper and Row, 1976).

43. "A Temperate Case," 95 n. 37.

44. Cf. my *God in Strength,* 170-201, and Borg's *Conflict, Holiness & Politics,* 259. Borg cites my position on Mark 9:1 (n. 93) in what precedes and my emphasis on the transcendence implied in Matt. 8:11, 12/Luke 13:28, 29, but not my exegesis of its transcendent meaning *as achieved by eschatology.*

Yet the relationship between the Kingdom and temporal futurity is not clear. Nothing suggests that it is to be soon. Moreover, though the coming of the many from the east and west is future, the Kingdom itself is not necessarily so, but may already "exist" as a realm beyond time, transcending time.[45]

The first sentence will only stand if its exact wording is observed: the kingdom and the future are evidently connected, although their exact relationship is not spelled out. *Borg implicitly acknowledges that the kingdom and the future are linked;* what he calls attention to is that a temporal sequence or calendar of the kingdom is not provided by Jesus' saying. He then behaves as if he has successfully argued against the future dimension of the saying's significance, which is not the case. In the second sentence, Borg observes that imminence is not suggested by the saying, which may be granted provided one recollects that *it also is not denied.* Borg simply abandons exegesis in his third sentence and speculates freely concerning the timeless nature of the kingdom without reference to the sayings of Jesus. His invocation of Smith's "primordial tradition," itself a debatable concept,[46] is used to reduce Jesus' teaching to a single "symbol for the experience of God in the other realm which is outside time."[47]

Before we proceed to discuss how an approach such as Borg's might continue to inform critical work, it is necessary to comment on the setting in which it was later developed, the "Jesus Seminar." In an account of the meetings of the seminar that were devoted to eschatology, James Williams approvingly refers to the work of Burton Mack, who in turn develops his position on the basis of three passages in the literature of Hellenistic Judaism.[48] Williams comments:

Mack is quite right in pointing out the rarity of the phrase "the

45. *Conflict, Holiness & Politics,* 259.

46. Scholars of religion have as a whole not accepted the hypothesis that religious experience remains constant as one moves from culture to culture. The contention that it does may be considered to be a kind of academic imperialism, since a scholar can only characterize "experience" on the basis of one's own culture.

47. *Conflict, Holiness & Politics,* 259, still commenting on Matt. 8:11, 12/Luke 13:28, 29!

48. The passages are Philo's *De specialibus legibus* 4.164; Wisdom 10:10; and *Sentences of Sextus* 311.

kingdom of God" apart from the Christian texts. In Jewish literature, we find the exact phrase only in the three instances cited above.[49]

Let us be clear: Mack is quite wrong, and his attempt to construe Jesus' preaching purely on the basis of Hellenistic antecedents only succeeds to the extent that Judaic texts that have long been known and studied are willfully ignored by scholars who should know better than to engage in such special pleading.[50]

The phrase "kingdom of heavens" in Rabbinic literature was long ago discussed as an antecedent of Jesus' teaching by T. W. Manson in his classic work *The Teaching of Jesus*.[51] Use of "heavens" instead of "God" corresponds exactly to the preferred usage in the Gospel according to Matthew and reflects the pious reticence in early Judaism to refer to God directly. No such reticence is apparent in the Targumim; the precise phrase "kingdom of God," *in Aramaic,* refers to God's own activity in vindicating his people. Recently, Anna Maria Schwemer has shown that the *Songs of Sabbath Sacrifice* from Qumran apply the language of "kingdom" to God's heavenly Temple.[52]

Good scholarship simply does not proceed by ignoring what has long been known and what the primary sources tell us. Although the emergence of North American contributors as genuine partners with their European colleagues can only be welcomed, the danger of provincialism has also emerged. It is as if a work must be recently published in English by one of the correct publishers for it to count as evidence

---

49. J. G. Williams, "Neither Here nor There: Between Wisdom and Apocalyptic in Jesus' Kingdom Sayings," *Forum* 5 (1989) 7-30. Williams himself comes to the conclusion that Mack's attempt to read Jesus' theology of the kingdom purely in terms of a Hellenistic understanding of wisdom does not succeed (pp. 9-24). Mack's "The Kingdom Sayings in Mark" appears in *Forum* 3 (1987) 3-47. For a suggestion that the phrase "kingdom of God" might be attested at Qumran, see R. Eisenman and M. Wise, *The Dead Sea Scrolls Uncovered* (Rockport: Element, 1992) 174.

50. For a considered appraisal of the Hellenistic sense of such usages, cf. K. W. Müller, "König und Vater. Streiflichter zur metaphorischen Rede über Gott in der Umwelt des Neuen Testaments," in M. Hengel and A. M. Schwemer (eds.), *Königsherrschaft Gottes und himmlischer Kult im Judentum, Christentum und in der hellenistichen Welt* (Wissenschaftliche Untersuchungen zum Neuen Testament 55; Tübingen: Mohr, 1991) 21-43.

51. *The Teaching of Jesus: Studies of Its Form and Content* (Cambridge: Cambridge University, 1955 [first edition 1931]) 116-141.

52. Schwemer, "Gott als König und seine Königsherrschaft in den Sabbatliedern aus Qumran," *Königsherrschaft Gottes und himmlischer Kult,* 45-118, here 48.

in the work of some scholars. If that is the price of a purely Hellenistic Jesus, only those who are disposed to accept the portrait on ideological grounds will be willing to pay it.

Williams's article is useful, not only because it identifies the sort of misinformation on which the "Jesus Seminar" sometimes proceeded, but also because it reveals the motivation for the attempt, in its response to the report on deliberations provided by James Butts:

> The unstated factor is that apocalyptic eschatology has become a burning issue in our time, especially for those biblical scholars who either have a "Bible belt" background or who must deal professionally with fundamentalists and dispensationalists. The element of ideology at work here, in my opinion, is that it is much easier to "save the text" (or *some* texts) and reinterpret the tradition if one comes up with a non-eschatological Jesus who is more congenial to the social location and professional functioning of the biblical scholar.[53]

As Williams goes on to say, Butts simply replaces conservative piety with the preferences of modern scholars and offers them as findings of research.[54] If Butts reports its discussions accurately, the Seminar confused eschatology and apocalyptic and eliminated them both from the portrait of Jesus in order to challenge modern fundamentalism. I have been a member of the Jesus Seminar for some time, and some of its findings are well worth considering, but the attempt by some of its members (including Marcus Borg) to write eschatology out of the record is misleading, as well as unsuccessful.

While Borg's thesis is too dependent on an outworn generalization regarding "the other world" to amount to an exegetical case, and while the Jesus Seminar was simply too confused to produce a plausible result, the deep unease with any rigid form of the eschatological consensus remains. The problem is that unease by itself is not a useful guide. During the course of discussion it has led to exaggeration time and again. Unhappiness with eschatology as the primary reference of the

---

53. "Neither Here nor There," pp. 25, 26. Williams is responding to J. R. Butts, "Probing the Poll: Jesus Seminar Results on the Kingdom Sayings," *Forum* 3 (1987) 98-128, and particularly to Butts's assertion that "for Jesus, the kingdom of God was *not* an eschatological nor an apocalyptic phenomenon" (Butts, 112).

54. Williams, "Neither Here nor There," 27 n. 44.

kingdom is easily converted into an equation of the kingdom with whatever the going orthodoxy is: the kingdom is the Church (so Carmignac), the kingdom is the Christ (so Dodd), the kingdom is the mystical experience of the sage Jesus (so Borg), or his philosophy in a Hellenistic key (so Mack).[55]

But the denial of eschatology, however it has been justified, has never prevailed. Whatever the force of a fashion might be, certain features of the evidence have proven to be recalcitrant, and they have never been successfully marginalized for long. The reference to the definitive future in many of Jesus' sayings, the expectation of final judgment in much of the literature of early Judaism, the hard fact of reference to the kingdom in Judaic writings (Aramaic, Greek, and Hebrew): those are basic data to be explained, not inconveniences that may be ignored.

Any attempt to ignore them brings about a predictable result. For every scholar who espouses a "non-eschatological" kingdom, there is sooner or later at least one who will call to mind the simple data that Weiss and Schweitzer emphasized. That is why the debate between eschatologists and those who have denied the eschatology of Jesus has marked time without advancing, in the manner of a metronome. Discussion has been so burdened by what we feel about Jesus' eschatology that it has failed to focus on what we can see of meanings beyond eschatology in Jesus' preaching.

As in so much else, Schweitzer's example is instructive. Having seen the eschatological dimension of Jesus' message, he then felt its ethical dimension. And he acted more on what he felt than on what he saw. We have already seen (pp. 6-16 above) how critical consideration has now mapped Jesus' ethics in a way that complements his eschatology. In other words, progress in understanding the kingdom is possible, not by denying eschatology as a reference of the kingdom, but by accepting that the kingdom may have dimensions alongside eschatology.[56]

An architect working today will use techniques, designs, and materials that were developed during the modern period, but the result is

55. Crossan's recent contribution may be regarded as a working out of Mack's thesis, at least insofar as it concerns the kingdom of God. Cf. J. D. Crossan, *The Historical Jesus: The Life of a Mediterranean Jewish Peasant* (San Francisco: Harper, 1991).

56. That now appears to be Borg's position, though he insists that he has not changed his mind; see his *Jesus in Contemporary Scholarship* (Valley Forge: Trinity Press International, 1994) 88.

likely to be "postmodern." The building, that is, will probably — and consciously — include features from earlier periods for practical and aesthetic reasons. In a similar way, exegetes of the kingdom must be prepared to be post-eschatological, to discover the lineaments of the meaning of the kingdom alongside eschatology.[57] The ethical dimension has become plain already, but its very existence suggests that, within the understanding of Jesus, other dimensions were operative as well.

Those dimensions of meaning, however, cannot be invented arbitrarily, nor is it sufficient to consider Jesus' sayings alone, apart from their context in what he actually did in the name of the kingdom. In order to understand the model of the kingdom that Jesus constructed, we need to appreciate how its dimensions were mapped in the Judaism of his time. That is the topic of the next chapter. On the basis of that consideration we will then, in the following chapters, focus on the model of the kingdom conveyed by Jesus' sayings and by his characteristic activities.

57. Schweitzer presents himself as a thoroughly modern thinker when he insists that one must conceive of Jesus' teaching as *either* eschatological *or* noneschatological. A post-eschatological orientation will help us move beyond that dichotomy.

CHAPTER 2

Mapping the Kingdom

The Book of Psalms

Introduction: God Far and Near in Early Judaism

The conviction that God is transcendent, beyond the terms of reference of what people see and imagine, is basic within the biblical tradition. It is the ultimate ground of the commandment against idolatry,[1] a proscription that lives on today in Judaism, Christianity, and Islam. The book of Deuteronomy (4:15-20) explains that God speaks to his people generally without granting a vision of himself, so that they do not confuse an image with the reality of God.[2]

But alongside the assertion of divine transcendence, the biblical tradition insists on God's nearness to his people. Juxtaposed, the two claims seem paradoxical. If God is beyond us, he is presumably remote, but the same book of Deuteronomy that insists that we have no image of God also claims that we have God's own voice in the book of Torah, which he gave to Moses; it is "in your mouth and in your heart, so that you may do it" (Deut. 30:10-14). Obeying the commandment is the means by which God's presence is realized. God is better put into prac-

---

1. See Exod. 20:4; Deut. 5:8.

2. The fact remains, of course, that the biblical tradition presents exceptional narratives of divine vision by particular individuals. See Exod. 24:10-11; 33:18-23; Isa. 6:1-5.

tice than he is imagined. He is far from our thoughts, but — in a telling metaphor — Deuteronomy pictures God's ways as circumcised in the hearts of his people (30:6). What they do, rather than what they think, is the only image of God that does not naturally slip in idolatry.

Deuteronomy also conveys a simple scheme of punishment and reward: if Israel obeys God's commands, they will know prosperity and see their enemies punished (30:1-10). The simplicity of that promise made it one of the dominant motifs of the Hebrew Bible. The hope of restoration as a consequence of obedience enabled Israel (or, at least, Judah, the southern kingdom) to recover from the destruction of the Temple in 587 BCE. The policy of exile that the Babylonians imposed should have destroyed the civilization of Jerusalem; the northern kingdom of Israel had perished at the hands of the Assyrians under the same policy a century and a half earlier. The Deuteronomic promise, woven not only into Deuteronomy itself, but into the fabric of the written Bible,[3] gave a fragile culture the power to survive the virtual certainty of extinction. The Temple was destroyed in 587 BCE, but then restored in 515 BCE. To speak in terms of the resurrection of a people would be no exaggeration of the importance of that event. It was possible only because Babylon fell to the Persians and because Persian policy toward the Jews oscillated between toleration and benign neglect.[4] At the same time, the restoration of the Temple could not have occurred without the powerful engine of hope that the Deuteronomic promise set to working.

The Deuteronomic scheme assured the survival of a people and its Mosaic book of the Torah. But it obviously could not determine the conditions of survival. Foreign occupation, disagreements among Jews, divisions in the priesthood, popular acceptance of customs condemned by the Torah: such were the realities of life in "restored" Israel. By the second century BCE, the Deuteronomic promise of prosperity in exchange for obedience to the Torah no longer seemed tenable in its original form.

Just that century saw the emergence of the book of Daniel. Daniel

3. The Hebrew Bible as we know it came into existence as a consequence of the destruction of the first Temple and the exile to Babylon. Among its basic components were the Deuteronomic edition of the Pentateuch and what is called the "Deuteronomistic History" of Israel after the occupation of Canaan, which is now represented in the books of Joshua, Judges, Samuel, and Kings.

4. See John Bright, *A History of Israel* (3rd ed., Philadelphia: Westminster, 1981) 360-372.

promises that "the God of heaven will raise up a kingdom that shall never be destroyed, and its rule[5] shall not be left to another people" (2:44). Within the book, it is clear that the kingdom is to appear definitively, that is, as part of an eschatological expectation of how human events are to end and how divine events are to supersede them. But the same work can also speak of the divine royalty in timeless terms: "His kingdom is an everlasting kingdom, and his dominion from generation to generation" (4:3; see also 4:34; 6:27). That is, the power of God's rule is eternal, although its disclosure in time is still to come and eagerly awaited.

When the kingdom of God is disclosed, it will be associated with the kingdom of an angelic figure like a person ("a son of man"), to whom dominion is given by God (Dan. 7:13, 14).[6] That figure, the source of the phrase "son of man" as an eschatological image, is part of the genuinely apocalyptic development of the book of Daniel. Here, a calendar of days is explicitly associated with the final, angelic intervention, which is to culminate in the resurrection (see Daniel 12). It is true that the phrase "kingdom of God" does not appear word for word in Daniel. But to insist on that point seems pedantic, since the term "kingdom" does appear with "his" in contexts in which the unequivocal antecedent is God. The concept of the kingdom is well represented by a variety of terms that are related to the root of the words "king" *(melekh)* and "rule as king" *(malakh)*. The book as a whole leaves no doubt: the concept of the kingdom was embedded in early Judaism's attempt to speak of the God who is both far and near.

The term "early Judaism" is used with reference to the period between the second century BCE and the second century CE. Early Judaism bridges Judaism as the national religion of Israel in the ancient period and Judaism as later defined by the Rabbis on the basis of the Mishnah (ca. 200 CE). Apocalyptic circles such as the one that produced the book of Daniel represent a type of response to the confused conditions after the restoration of the Temple, conditions that seemed to disappoint the classic form of the Deuteronomic promise. The outcome

---

5. The term here is *malkhuthah,* a king's hegemony, which is the basic reference of "kingdom" *(malkhuth).* The abstract noun is related to *melekh* ("king") and to *malakh* ("to rule as king").

6. Cf. B. Chilton, "The Son of Man: Human and Heavenly," in *The Four Gospels: 1992* (Festschrift for F. Neirynck), ed. F. van Segbroeck, C. M. Tuckett, G. van Belle, and J. Verheyden (BETL 100; Leuven, 1992) 203-218.

of obedience, as in Deuteronomy, is no longer immediate prosperity; for Daniel, attentive patience is the key to rewards that are not available within the world as we know it.

Other types of response to the confused conditions of restored Israel were also represented in early Judaism. Among priestly groups in charge of the Temple (such as the Sadducees) it was held that the continued operation of the cult, even under the auspices of the Romans, was the necessary condition of God's approval of his people. The Essenes, on the other hand, envisaged their control of a new order in the Temple as part of their apocalyptic triumph over all the sons of darkness, non-Jewish and Jewish alike. The Pharisees were less radical in their separation from other Jews and their insistence on a new order, but they did elaborate particular conditions of the purity that they held God demanded of Israel.

The variety among these groups is so stunning that some of the features that united them may be overlooked. The covenant with Moses, the privileged status of the Hebrew Bible, the centrality of the Temple, the hope that the promise to David's house would be realized in some form: such were the constitutional elements of early Judaism. The different groups also evolved a vocabulary of the near and far God. In the critical circumstances of early Judaism, in which the Deuteronomic promise of prosperity in exchange for obedience no longer seemed tenable, considerable sophistication was necessary to explain how the God who was removed from human conceptions was also near at hand in an effective way. Early Judaic conceptions are reflected in the latest books of the Bible, as well as in the Apocrypha and Pseudepigrapha,[7] the Targums (Aramaic paraphrases of the Hebrew Bible),[8] and certain portions of other Rabbinic literature.[9]

One might refer to God under the aspect of his "Shekhinah," his festive presence in the sacrificial worship that took place in the Temple.

7. See James H. Charlesworth (ed.), *The Old Testament Pseudepigrapha* (Garden City: Doubleday, 1983, 1985).

8. "The Aramaic Bible," a series that began to appear in 1987 under the general editorship of Martin McNamara (Collegeville: Liturgical Press/Edinburgh: Clark), is now complete. The richest resource for students of the New Testament is the Targum of Isaiah; cf. B. Chilton, *The Isaiah Targum: Introduction, Translation, Apparatus, and Notes* (The Aramaic Bible; 1987).

9. See J. Neusner, *The Pharisees: Rabbinic Perspectives* (Studies in Ancient Judaism 1; Hoboken: Ktav, 1973).

The term derives from the verb *shakhan,* which means "dwell in a tent" or "set up a tent." The verb is used to speak of God's presence with his people during the exodus, as a pillar of fire by night and a pillar of cloud by day (Exod. 24:16-18; 13:21-22). Both images are evocative of sacrifice in the Temple, where smoke billowed by day over the altar and embers glowed through the night. The point of the imagery in the book of Exodus is that God was with his people from the beginning of their existence just as he was available in the Temple. There was his "Shekhinah"; he was pleased to enjoy the presence of his people in the Temple and to make his own presence felt there in a way he did nowhere else.

God might also be known, as is also the case in the book of Exodus, under the aspect of his "glory" (*kabhod* in Hebrew, *yeqar* in Aramaic). Although the etymology of the Hebrew word has to do with "weight," in reference to God it applies to the radiant splendor that is the divine property alone. Because glory belongs truly to God, sitting in majesty upon his throne, he can also dispense it to those who turn to him in obedience (see Exod. 24:5-18).

The list of words and phrases used in early Judaism to refer to various aspects of God's activity may easily be extended.[10] In each case, however, the purpose of such language[11] is to preserve the biblical insistence that God is transcendent in regard to human conceptions but effective in regard to human behavior. In other words, the transcendence at issue is dynamic and cannot be conveyed by referring only to the supposed remoteness of God.

"Shekhinah" preserves the paradox of the near and far God by speaking of his enjoyment of his people within a Temple in which he was not visually depicted for worshipers. They were to conceive of his pleasure without the benefit of imagining him as eating, drinking, or reveling. Similarly, whether they were in the Temple or away from it, their obedience was said to provide access to the "glory" of a throne of unspeakable majesty. But that splendor ultimately shielded them from seeing God, because such a vision would ordinarily mean death (see Exod. 33:20).

Just as "Shekhinah" refers to God's dwelling in the Temple and

---

10. Cf. B. Chilton, *The Glory of Israel: The Theology and Provenience of the Isaiah Targum* (Journal for the Study of the Old Testament Supplement 23; Sheffield: JSOT, 1982).

11. Technically, terms of this sort are *theologoumena* — ways of speaking of God.

"glory" to the majesty of his throne, so "kingdom" implies a particular sphere of concern. The conception of God ruling from his seat of power might be used, as in the book of Daniel, to speak of divine intervention in this world or of the eternal force of that power in itself. The particular emphasis varied among the different circles of early Judaism.

The Pharisees and their successors, the Rabbis who were responsible for the formation of the Mishnah, spoke of the kingdom as a focus of obedience. For them, to recite the classic confession "Hear, O Israel, the LORD our God is one LORD . . ." (Deut. 6:4-9) was to "take on the yoke of the kingdom" (see Mishnah *Berakhoth* 2:2). Their picture of royal power was connected with the conviction that God was to be known and the life of Israel realized by means of the Torah given to Moses and articulated by the Rabbis themselves.

In the Targums, the influence of the Rabbis was less dominant. Although Rabbis were involved in the formulation of the Targums as they may be read today, the Targums also reflect the local customs of congregations of Jews who met in synagogues and heard the Scriptures in Aramaic. As a result, the kingdom in the Targumim does not accord completely with the kingdom in the Mishnah. Instead, "kingdom" is used in the Aramaic rendering when the Hebrew text speaks of God himself intervening on behalf of his people. For example, when, as part of the comforting news of God's victory in Isaiah 40, the cities of Judah are to be told (40:9) "Behold your God," that triumphant announcement becomes in the Targum, "The kingdom of your God is revealed." When God appears "in strength" (so Targum Isa. 40:10) to vindicate his own, that for the Targums is the kingdom of God.

The scrolls of Qumran represent yet another idiom of the kingdom. Neither the focus of obedience nor the preferred means of speaking of divine intervention, the kingdom is in the scrolls the circle of the heavenly host that gathers to worship God (see *Songs of Sabbath Sacrifice* 3:24-26).[12] In the view of the Essenes,[13] the community of their covenant joined themselves with the angels in worship, so that the

---

12. To consult the passage, see C. A. Newsome, *Songs of the Sabbath Sacrifice: A Critical Edition* (Harvard Semitic Studies 27; Atlanta: Scholars, 1985).

13. The Essenes were most likely those behind the establishment of the collection of scrolls; see Todd S. Beall, *Josephus' Description of the Essenes Illustrated by the Dead Sea Scrolls* (Society of New Testament Studies Monograph Series 58; Cambridge: Cambridge University, 1988).

reference of the kingdom certainly was not removed from how God might be known by his people. Still, the emphasis as compared to that of the Mishnah and Targumim is distinctively heavenly. Craig Evans has shown that phrases in the *Songs of Sabbath Sacrifice* such as "your kingdom," "his kingdom," and "kingdom of the king of all the gods" refer to the celestial aspects of God's rule. He cites one passage that is redolent of that reference, in which the angelic company around God's throne is called "the chiefs of the realm of the holy ones of the king of holiness in all the heights of the sanctuary of his glorious kingdom" (4Q405 23 ii 1-2).[14]

Alongside the distinctive usages of the Mishnah, the Targumim, and the scrolls of Qumran, there are the equally characteristic usages in the literature of Hellenistic Judaism. Here, the language emphasizes the eternity of God's kingdom, but it is not the eternity of God in himself or of the heavenly worship of God. The point is rather God's providential ordering of the creation, which is the reward of the righteous (see Wisdom 10:10). The world is held to reflect his kingdom, in the reasoned plan he put together by means of his Wisdom. Wisdom herself, of course, is personified in the literature, so that the philosophical power of God is at issue throughout.

Each of the usages of "kingdom" specified here has been compared with sayings of Jesus. The results have proved illuminating, but at each point differences are at least as important as similarities. T. W. Manson explored the comparison with the rabbinic "yoke of the kingdom," but he emphasized that the kingdom for Jesus was not the known quantity that the Rabbis presupposed, but involved a personal relationship with God.[15] Jesus in Manson's analysis called for loyalty to the kingdom as much as the Rabbis did, but without pursuing their virtual equation of the kingdom with the Torah.

Similarly, I have observed that the Targumim share Jesus' close identification of the kingdom with God himself. But the Targumim restrict the usage to the final phase of God's activity of rewarding and punishing, and they assume that the national boundaries of Israel will largely determine who is to be rewarded and who punished. Jesus'

---

14. C. A. Evans, *Jesus and His Contemporaries* (Arbeiten zur Geschichte des Antiken Judentums und des Urchristentums 25; Leiden: Brill, 1995) 150-152.

15. See T. W. Manson, *The Teaching of Jesus: Studies of Its Form and Content* (Cambridge: Cambridge University, 1955) 131-135.

characteristic usage was less finite in terms of a specific phase of divine revelation, and his definition of who belonged to the people of God was so loose that it caused controversy.[16] He compared the kingdom to a feast to which the invitations were already issued, and issued to unlikely recipients (Matt. 22:1-14/Luke 14:15-24).

More recent comparisons with the usage of Jesus involving the scrolls of Qumran and the literature of Hellenistic Judaism have not been pursued as completely as earlier analyses of the Targumim and Rabbinic literature. But a similar pattern, one of partial agreement and crucial disagreement, is emerging. Jesus, like the Essenes, spoke of the majesty of God when he referred to the kingdom.[17] But he did not share their view that worship in the Temple was to be replaced by a totally new order, one that the final battle between the sons of light and the sons of darkness was to realize. The Essene focus on the kingdom as the heavenly Temple — as God's sphere of sovereignty where alone he was known as king — was therefore not shared by Jesus. He spoke more easily of the kingdom as within nature. The immediacy with which he referred to the kingdom also sets him apart from the usage of Hellenistic Judaism,[18] where the emphasis is more philosophical, focused on the total pattern of the created order as ruled providentially.

The language of the kingdom was obviously varied in early Judaism. There were several distinctive usages of the concept, and Jesus' accorded completely with no single one of them. His understanding of the kingdom cannot be appreciated by supposing that he simply adopted any of the definitions that have been surveyed. Those who applied the concept, such as Jesus, did so with their own particular meanings. It has been plausibly supposed, for example, that those who advocated revolt against Roman rule did so by means of an appeal to the kingdom of God, taken as a political theocracy. The revolutionaries left behind no literary remains that permit us to prove that argument, but it is quite probable.

16. See B. Chilton, *A Galilean Rabbi and His Bible: Jesus' Use of the Interpreted Scripture of His Time* (Wilmington: Glazier, 1984) 58-63.

17. See A. M. Schwemer, "Gott als König und seine Königsherrschaft in den Sabbatliedern aus Qumran," in M. Hengel and A. M. Schwemer (eds.), *Königsherrschaft Gottes und himmlicher Kult im Judentum, Urchristentum und in der hellenistichen Welt* (Wissenschaftliche Untersuchungen zum Neuen Testament 55; Tübingen: Mohr, 1991) 45-118.

18. Contrast the treatment of the question by B. Mack in *A Myth of Innocence: Mark and Christian Origins* (Philadelphia: Fortress, 1988).

In order to appreciate any of the distinctive understandings of the kingdom in early Judaism, Jesus' included, it is necessary to step back and consider the broader conception of God as king that occasioned the language of the kingdom of God. Among all the sources, the book of Psalms is the richest in its presentation of the divine kingship. The Psalms were used in the context of worship in the Temple, by priests and Israelites alike; that is one reason that their language echoes again and again in the later sources of Judaism. But the more profound reason for the resonance of their language is that they develop a coherent manner of speaking of God as king. They speak of the dimensions of God's rule, so that later usages could map their own models of the kingdom along those dimensions.[19]

The Dimensions of the Kingdom in the Book of Psalms

The book of Psalms is a collection of various materials used during worship in the Temple that were later edited and extended in order to attempt to regulate worship there. The period after the Second Temple was dedicated (in 515 BCE) was fraught with conflict in Judaism because neither the priesthood nor the monarchy was the stable institution it had once been. Collections such as the book of Psalms represent attempts to establish a consensus of practice within the worship of Israel for priests and laity alike. The history of the development of reference to God as king in the Psalms is analyzed below in Appendix A. The purpose for the moment is not to review all the usages in their appropriate sequence; that is the concern of the appendix. Here, the concern is to consider the conception of Psalms as a whole. As Israel drew together for sacrificial worship in the Temple, what was the common understanding of the divine kingship involved there according to the conception of the Psalms?

In Psalms we must reckon with a much more nuanced application

---

19. Following recent developments in linguistic philosophy, we might say that Psalms establishes the setting in life within which language of God's kingship was sensible. Once that basic pattern of language was established, particular models of the kingdom could evolve at a later stage. Cf. G. L. Hagberg, *Meaning and Interpretation: Wittgenstein, Henry James, and Literary Knowledge* (Ithaca: Cornell University, 1994).

of a language of kingship to God than the modern fixation on eschatology would allow. The assertion of God as king refers normally to his majesty as the source and power of the creation itself, to the splendor of the forces at his command, to his rule on behalf of the people he chooses to call his own. Those principal aspects — power within the world, glorious splendor at the divine center, and sovereignty over the people of God — are automatically invoked when divine kingship is at issue. One or more of them may bear now more, now less emphasis, but to speak of God as king within the biblical tradition means that he is in charge of the world, that he is glorious, that his people attend to him and he to them. And Psalms sets the pace of that usage, in speaking persistently of God reigning *(malakh),* acting as king *(melekh).*

If God reigns, if the LORD of Israel is indeed the master of creation, glorious in his court, and determinative in the lives of his people, then how is his kingship known? The fundamental sense of the metaphor of God as king involves not so much a place as an activity, God's royal disclosure of his might. But even an activity needs to be located in order to be appreciated. Events, as well as places, have coordinates that enable one to engage with them. In its fulsome language of the divine kingship, the book of Psalms established five coordinates or dimensions of the kingdom, and it does so in language that became classic within the biblical tradition.

The Eschatological Coordinate

The first coordinate of which we will speak is the dimension of eschatology. It is not the most prominent; all five are invoked with approximately equal emphasis. But the contemporary debate concerning eschatology may be largely resolved by reference to Psalms, because the kingdom is portrayed as so near in time as to be present, and yet ultimate from the point of view of full disclosure (96:10):

> Say among the nations that the LORD reigns.
> The world is established, so as not to move:
> he will judge the peoples with equity.

Psalm 96 establishes as its context God's sovereign power over the creation as a whole, and the extent of God's rule is taken as the occasion to stress that his majesty is to be made known among those outside Israel. All the peoples are to know the truth that is now celebrated and sung in the Temple.

The whole earth is called in Psalm 96 to sing a new song to the LORD, to recount his glory and his wonderful deeds among the nations (vv. 1-3). The LORD's status as the creator of the heavens is stressed at the expense of the gods of the peoples (v. 5),[20] so that majesty and splendor are before him (in heaven) and strength and beauty are in his sanctuary (v. 6). The "tribes of the peoples" (v. 7)[21] are on that basis commanded to acknowledge the LORD by bringing offerings to his Temple: all the earth is to writhe before him (vv. 7-9).

The next phase of the Psalm (beginning with v. 10, quoted above) is particularly telling for an understanding of the divine kingdom on the basis of the book of Psalms generally. The Psalmic theology of Zion as God's chosen place is well known and is often invoked when the cosmological aspect of divine rule is also at issue. The idea is that Zion, as God's own abode (see, for example, Isa. 8:18 and Ps. 43:3), should be understood as the very center of the creation (see, for example, Ezek. 38:12 and Ps. 125:1).[22] But in addition to that motif, an eschatological emphasis appears in Psalm 96 and relates the universal claim of God's rule to the universal judgment that is to come. The local aspect of the sanctuary in Zion is not treated as in the least inconsistent with the eschatological emphasis. On the contrary, the sanctuary's strength and beauty reflect the divine majesty and splendor (v. 6): Zion is precisely the point at which God's sovereignty is recognized and the focus from which the divine sovereignty will radiate.

Although Psalm 96 brings the eschatological dimension to paradigmatic expression, that dimension is also apparent in Psalms 44, 47, 96, and 98. The coordinate of time involves an awareness that God's rule may be known temporally, as revealed now in Zion and within creation itself. The existence of life and the sacrificial worship of Israel

20. For the same motif see 97:7.

21. The phrase is striking (cf. Ps. 22:28) and intimates what will be discussed more fully below: the inclusion of the peoples in the acknowledgment of the God of Israel attributes to them a social structure comparable to Israel's. They become like Israel in recognizing God and joining in his worship.

22. See G. Fohrer, *Theological Dictionary of the New Testament* VII, ed. G. Friedrich, tr. G. W. Bromiley (Grand Rapids: Eerdmans, 1979) 293-319.

(which deploys that life in its pure form) together attest God's sovereign power. But together with an awareness of God's rule in its temporality, there is also an anticipation that it will be recognized among non-Israelites. That is, for God truly to be the king of creation and of history, an ultimate disclosure of his power is required. The eschatological coordinate of the kingdom is the tension between its temporality and its ultimacy, between that of which one can be aware and that which one can only anticipate. Within the theology of the Psalms, there can be no absolute contrast between the kingdom as present and the kingdom as coming: the future crowns what is now, just as what is now sets the throne for hope in the future.

The Transcendent Coordinate

In modern usage, we speak of transcendence in the abstract sense, to refer to God as above — and independent of — the universe. But "to transcend" at base refers to action and movement, to surpassing a physical limit or boundary. As the entry in *The Oxford English Dictionary* shows, theologians have tended to refer to transcendence in its most abstract and general sense. That is unfortunate for our inquiry, because transcendence in its basic, spatial sense emerges as an important coordinate of the kingdom in the book of Psalms. Abstraction only clouds the matter.

Psalm 145 anticipates the universal range of God's rule. The psalm assumes the usual setting of Israel's praise in the Temple, but now it is hoped that every part of the creation will come to acknowledge what is known there (vv. 10-13):

> All your creatures will give you thanks, LORD,
> and your faithful will bless you;
> they will speak of the glory of your kingdom
> and tell of your might,
> to make your mighty deeds known to the sons of men,
> and the glorious splendor of his kingdom.
> Your kingdom is an everlasting kingdom,
> and your rule in every generation.

All his creatures are to give thanks to the LORD, but it is his faithful in particular who are said to bless him. They speak of the glory of his kingdom and his might, making them known to the sons of men, in that his kingdom and dominion are eternal. What is rehearsed in the Temple, the "strength of the fearful acts" of God, is to be acknowledged by humanity as a whole (v. 6).

Psalm 145 anticipates a universal acknowledgment of the kingdom because, in its conception, the divine rule even now extends to every place and creature. God supports those who are fallen or distressed and nourishes every living thing (vv. 14-16): the LORD is righteous and faithful in all (v. 17, cf. vv. 7, 9), near and responsive to all who call on him (vv. 18-20a). For that reason, the force of his judgment is to extend to everyone, both to those who love him and to the wicked (v. 20).

The final image of the psalm (v. 21), that all flesh should bless the holy name of the LORD, is an ideal realized for the moment only in the place of his holiness. But the coordinate of transcendence makes the locality of the Temple a model for what the entire creation is to be. What is local, in Zion, is the pattern for what is to be universal, throughout creation.

The common denominator in the recognition of God in his Temple and the universal praise that is to come is the reality of God's power. That power is palpable in the ordering of creation, but it is one day to be fully public knowledge. God's deeds and acts, in Israel's history and in the forces of nature, bring about an awareness of his majesty. The transcendence of God's rule, beyond the bounds of Israel and the Temple, in no sense weakens the specificity of Israel's God. On the contrary, the kingdom now known locally is to be praised everywhere. The immanent power of God, today recognized only in the Temple, is to be known by all God's creatures. For that reason, psalms that articulate the coordinate of transcendence (see Psalms 22, 93, and 145) stress that the kingdom is a matter of dynamic power in the universe and in people's experience.

The transcendent coordinate of the kingdom is rooted in the nature of divine power. Because no limit can be imagined on the force of God as he orders the universe and sustains his people, so his kingdom must be understood to be limitless. It is there already, immanent in the life of every living thing; from the perspective of Psalms, the mystery is only that there are those who would not acknowledge the kingdom. But for every instance of such resistance, there is more power to come, until all flesh will celebrate the source of its being.

The Coordinate of Judgment

Judgment is implicit in the kingdom because what is wicked in this world must be overcome if God's final (eschatological) power is to permeate his creation (transcending every boundary that would limit the recognition of his might). The first two coordinates of the kingdom for that reason include the third as their necessary correlate, although the ethical demands involved in judgment distinguish the third coordinate from the others. The kingdom is ever righteous, but attains to a consummation (Ps. 10:15-16):

> Break the arm of the wicked and evil;
> search out his wickedness until it cannot be found!
> The LORD is king forever and ever;
> the nations perish from his earth!

The punishment of the wicked is the dark side of the establishment of the poor; the vindication of the meek, the fatherless, and the oppressed (vv. 17, 18a) requires a reversal in the fortunes of those who do evil. Their power must be removed so that they no longer strike terror in the hearts of the righteous (v. 18b).

The imagery of Psalm 10 is personal, in its complaint against the deliberate greed and violence of the wicked (vv. 1-11, 13), against a desire for gain that actually takes pleasure in the harm it inflicts on others. But the personal language is not limited; it is used in a much broader context.

Psalm 10 was directly associated with Psalm 9: each line of the two together begins with the successive letter of the Hebrew alphabet. This acrostic shows that Psalm 9 provides the natural context for the meaning of Psalm 10. They are a single unit in the Septuagint. In Psalm 9, it is plain that the form of individual lament is applied to national disaster: the vindication of Israel at the expense of non-Jewish nations is expressly celebrated (see 9:5, 6).

In Psalms 9 and 10, God is asked to act in conformity to his own nature, and therefore to reverse injustice. In both psalms, God is referred to as king (9:7-8; 10:16) in a confident claim of divine sovereignty that effectively identifies those outside Israel with the wicked. The language of royal rule is naturally invoked. The association of that rule with complete triumph over the enemies of Israel is a regular feature of the understanding of God's kingship in the book of Psalms generally.

Two features of the coordinate of judgment should be distinguished. The first is a necessary outcome of the very concept of the divine kingdom, while the second seems to be a function of the social setting of the Psalms. The distinction between these two features will enable us more clearly to understand variant understandings of the kingdom among those who were familiar with the book of Psalms.

The conditions of this world, understood as the social order that people construct in any time, are incompatible with the rule of God. That is as evident as the greed and violence that are obvious and ambient within human culture. Some societies may seem more just than others, and a given society might grow or decay in its claim to justice, but the nature of God's justice is radically different from the qualities of human justice; "my ways are not your ways" is a formulation that the book of Isaiah comes to at the climax of an eschatological section (Isa. 55:8b); it expresses a basic principle of Judaic (and therefore Christian) eschatology.

The exaltation of God's ways is sandwiched between a call for the wicked to forsake his way (Isa. 55:7) and confident assurance that the disclosure of God's purpose is as sure as the fructifying power of the rain (vv. 10-11). In Psalm 10, then, a necessary correlate of eschatology comes to expression: if God's will is to triumph, those who are antagonistic to it must either be converted or destroyed.

But Psalm 9–10 is unlike Isaiah 55 in its identification of who precisely the wicked are. In Isaiah 55, the (non-Jewish) nations are to stream into Jerusalem, startled at David's vindication by God, the holy one of Israel (v. 5). In Psalm 9–10, the nations are the enemy, only to be blotted out in everlasting ruins (see Ps. 9:5-6). The difference in time between the relevant sections in Isaiah[23] and Psalms is not great.[24] Although God's elimination of the wicked is a common coordinate of his kingdom, there was a variety of understandings of who and what were to be eliminated.

In Psalm 97, the target of judgment is idolatry, so that the threat of punishment is relevant to Israelites and non-Israelites alike (although usually it is more threatening to the latter). Psalm 103 is positive in its

---

23. Chapters 40–55 are usually dated in the sixth century BCE; see J. L. McKenzie, *Second Isaiah* (Anchor Bible; Garden City: Doubleday, 1968).

24. See Appendix A, where Psalms 9, 10, 44, 74, 95, 114, and 149 are assigned to a somewhat later period of national restoration.

imagery of judgment: its emphasis is so consumed with the vindication of those who fear the LORD (vv. 6-18) that there is no time to speak of the punishment of their oppressors. The balance between positive and negative constructions of judgment, between vindication and punishment, varies from psalm to psalm, just as the definition of who is to be punished changes. Judgment, that is, like eschatology and transcendence, is not a fixed theme; nor is it an expectation of a single scenario of vindication and punishment: judgment is rather a genuine coordinate of the kingdom, defined by the demand for justice in the present and anticipation of perfection in the future. Along that coordinate, the definition, nature, and timing of judgment are all matters that need to be specified by whoever speaks of the kingdom.

The Coordinate of Purity

Psalm 24 poses a question that is central to the religion of Israel as reflected in the biblical tradition: "Who will ascend the mount of the LORD, and who will stand in his holy place?" (v. 3). The assumption behind the question is that Zion is God's mountain, the place that he has assigned himself (see also Ps. 15:1 and the discussion of Psalm 96 above). For that reason, sacrifice offered there (and *only* there) is pleasing to God. But what is offered must be pure; it must be brought by a pure people and sacrificed by a pure, designated priesthood. Purity in Israel was required of every person, thing, and action associated with the Temple.[25] Psalm 24 assumes all that. In this assumption it also suggests — by posing the question that it poses — that something more than conventional practice is required.

The psalm, which is emphatic in its portrait of God as king (vv. 7-10), does not delay in specifying what that something more is (v. 4):

> The one who is innocent of hands and pure of heart,
> has not lifted up his soul to vanity,
> and has not sworn deceitfully.

25. For further discussion, see my *The Temple of Jesus: His Sacrificial Program within a Cultural History of Sacrifice* (University Park: Pennsylvania State University, 1992) 45-67.

It is plain that any rigid differentiation between ethical and cultic regulations is formally dissolved here. Although such a distinction is current in modern theology, in Psalm 24 the point is that purity is effected by one's ethical behavior as well as by the gestures of purification (such as bathing and abstention from sexual intercourse) that were conventionally associated with ascending the mount of the Temple.

The coordinate of judgment, as we have seen, seals the importance of ethics within the purview of the kingdom by insisting on the final distinction that is to be made between righteousness and wickedness. The coordinate of purity presents ethics as crucial in the present, because what one does influences one's immediate access to the divine presence. Clean hands and a pure heart are the conditions in which blessing and vindication may be realized (vv. 5-6), because one is then prepared to meet the LORD in his coming (vv. 7-10).

Purity is the condition — not only the physical and social condition, but the moral condition as well — in which one is fit to stand in the holy place. Those who are clean in that comprehensive sense are enabled to encounter God as he appropriates as his own what is offered purely. It becomes holy, God's own, because he accepts it. The coordinate of purity is correlative with the coordinate of judgment, in that both are concerned with behavior. But where judgment is a matter of the outcome of action for the person who acts, the outcome of purity is God's actual appropriation of what God has designated in advance as belonging to him.

Purity in the inclusive sense, involving conventional cleanness and the ethical removal of oneself from anything evil, is what enables those who are righteous to enter the house of God (see Ps. 5:7), to be heard by the divine king (Ps. 5:2). The tenor of Psalm 5 is especially cognate with the abhorrence of wickedness within the coordinate of judgment (see pp. 36-38). But purity can also be celebrated for its own sake (much as righteousness can; see Psalm 103 as discussed above, pp. 37-38). Psalm 149 portrays the festive celebration of the children of Zion in their king (v. 2): song, dance, victory, the luxury of couches at mealtime (vv. 1, 3-5), all are emblems of God's pleasure in his people (v. 4), a pleasure that enables them to triumph over their enemies (vv. 6-9). But whether conceived of negatively as distance from uncleanness and immorality, or positively as pure celebration before the LORD, purity is the condition that anticipates holiness, and the anticipation involves an engagement with God's presence in the Temple.

The coordinate of purity involves the promise that people who are suitably prepared will enter God's presence, the place of his Temple, and that in that holy space God himself will enter. One stands where the king of glory is himself to come (Ps. 24:3, 7). Purity necessarily implies a displacement of oneself toward God in anticipation of God's responsive unveiling of his holiness. From the point of view of both the person who purifies and the God who enters purified space, purity envisages movement, a pilgrimage to the shrine where God himself also intends to be a pilgrim.

The Coordinate of Radiance

Once realized, purity changes the nature of the place where it is achieved. The people, when they have been prepared, become fully (not only potentially) the children of God, and the hidden God is revealed in his holiness. Within the book of Psalms, the Temple is the only place where this double transformation of Israel and Israel's God might occur. Because the place of the transformation is known and may be visited from the side of the divine as well as from the side of the human, it is the source of the only change that matters. There, and there alone, people are human and God is holy.

Because the place of this transformation is clearly identified as the Temple, it is a stable source of powerful change. The kingdom that is associated uniquely with two particular locations, Zion and heaven, is to take up all peoples (obviously apart from the wicked) in its disclosure. In Psalm 47, all the peoples are to acclaim that the LORD is "great king over all the earth" (vv. 1-2).

Although the horizon of the claim of divine sovereignty is without limit in Psalm 47, the focus of the kingdom is well defined. God acquired an inheritance *for Jacob* at the expense of those peoples whom God subdued, yet those peoples are to praise him together with Israel in the acclamation of the LORD with shouting and the sound of the horn (vv. 3-5). The site of the musical recognition of God as "our king" (v. 6) is evidently the Temple, but he is also "king of all the earth" (v. 7). He both rules over the nations (v. 8a) and is installed on his holy throne (v. 8b), Mount Zion itself. Those "nations" (cf. v. 8a) are in a position of awed impotence as a result of Israel's triumph, and there is never any doubt about the preference for Israel.

Nonetheless, Psalm 47 ends with an emphatic assertion that "the shields of the earth are God's" (v. 9). That is, the peoples who are called to join in songs of joy at the triumph of the divine king include the nations over whom he rules, whose power he takes over. The transcendent coordinate, which we have already discussed (pp. 34-35), involves the reach of God's power into the whole of creation; the present concern involves the conscious devotion of the peoples to God. It is a matter of the recognition of the righteousness of God's power among those from whom such recognition is unexpected in the usual course of things.

The language of Psalm 47 is again evocative of how the recognition of God is to radiate from Zion when it identifies "the people of the God of Abraham" together with "the nobles of the peoples" (v. 9):

> The nobles of the peoples are gathered,
>   the people of the God of Abraham;
> for the shields of the earth are God's.
> He is highly exalted!

Israel is the nucleus of the larger group of those who recognize the God of Jacob. From its center, the power of the kingdom is to radiate outward to include peoples beyond the usual range of Israel within its recognition. And just as purity involves a double transformation, of the human and of the divine, so the coordinate of radiance entails a double movement: the power of the kingdom radiates outward, and the recognition of the peoples radiates *toward* the kingdom.

The radiance of the kingdom, then, is both what proceeds from that source and what is given in response to the kingdom, especially from those outside Israel. The affective result of the recognition of the kingdom in Psalm 47 is positive: all the peoples join in joyful praise, even musical praise. But in Psalm 48, the affective involvement of the (non-Jewish) kings is as emphatically negative as non-Jewish response is positive in Psalm 47: they see, and flee in shattered panic (48:4-7). Those responsible for the resistance to radiance in the present are ultimately called to account. No clearer indication could be imagined that the coordinate of radiation does not contradict, but complements, the coordinate of judgment. The force of the kingdom is such that, willingly or unwillingly, recognition of its primacy will follow.

Because the recognition of the kingdom, the coordinate of radiation, follows inevitably from the nature of the kingdom itself, it can also be conceived of as already achieved. The sons of God in the heavenly court can be pictured as giving God glory in celebration of his power in the creation (Psalm 29). That picture of the overwhelming power of God can also be developed by means of the imagery of nature itself trembling at the divine presence (Psalm 114), although the sustaining force of God might also be emphasized (Psalm 145). Because the kingdom is God's, its recognition is ineluctable. That is the logic of the coordinate of radiance.

Visions of the Kingdom

The five coordinates are so closely related within the language of the kingdom that one example from the Psalms might be used to illustrate more than one coordinate.[26] That tends to confirm that we have here identified genuinely *systemic* dimensions of meaning for the kingdom: speaking of the kingdom along the lines of one coordinate leads naturally, and sometimes inevitably, to an assertion along the lines of another coordinate, or of several other coordinates. Referring to the kingdom within the world of the Psalms, and therefore within early Judaism, invokes a system of meaning that explains the place of Israel in the world and before God. Of course, the coordinates determine how the kingdom will be spoken of, but not what will be said of it or how exactly it will be described along the lines of each coordinate. A given speaker or circle of usage would develop a particular understanding of the content and character of the kingdom, appropriate to the historical conditions involved.

A priestly circle could emphasize the irreducible importance of Zion as the geographical focus of the kingdom (within the transcendent coordinate), the place on earth where heaven chose to dwell. A revolutionary circle could accord first importance to the subjugation of the nations, whose power would then radiate toward its divine center (the coordinate of radiance). Pharisees might start with the coordinate of purity, Essenes and other apocalyptic groups with the coordinate of eschatology, students of Hellenistic Wisdom with the coordinate of judgment.

26. When the wider context of each passage is considered, this observation becomes all the more valid.

Each vision of the kingdom carries with it a distinctive program of systematic practice. The priestly obsession with the Temple should not be reduced to a matter of self-interest: the sanctuary was for committed priests and those who agreed with them the focal point of the kingdom. Likewise, a revolutionary inspired by the kingdom is less a political actor in his own mind than an agent of the divine glory. The purity espoused by the Pharisees is motivated not by a love of legalism but by the understanding of where God is pleased to reveal himself. Apocalyptists construct calendars less to compute the end than to anticipate the beginning of the full disclosure of the divine rule.

The variety of conceptions of the kingdom in early Judaism cannot be grasped adequately by means of the true and obvious assertion that definitions differed from group to group. The character of the variety involved is in fact far more interesting. A group evolves its distinctive vision of the kingdom out of its application of a common language of the divine rule (best reflected in Psalms) to its particular social circumstances. The result is a variety that may be mapped systematically by means of reference to the coordinates of the kingdom that have been described.

Within each coordinate, the first pole designates the kingdom as it impinges upon those who might respond to it; for them, the kingdom appears (1) near, (2) powerful, (3) demanding, (4) pure, and (5) associated with Zion in particular. The second pole of each dimension designates the goal implicit within the kingdom, the (1) final, (2) immanent, (3) faultless, (4) holy, and (5) inclusive reality it promises to be. The fulfillment of the kingdom is not only a question of time, but involves the fulfillment of time together with the fulfillment of place, the fulfillment of ethics, the fulfillment of purity, and the fulfillment of the kingdom's recognition.

The kingdom of God is a scandal for modern thinking not only because it purports to be final. The kingdom is indeed eschatological in respect of time, as Weiss and Schweitzer maintained, but also transcendent in respect of place (in Zion, in heaven, and everywhere), perfect in respect of action, sacred in its purity, and all-embracing in its choice of Israel. Within the Psalms, the assertion of God as king refers normally to his rule on behalf of his people, as present and to come, intervening and yet all-pervasive, demanding righteousness and anticipating perfection, requiring a purity cognate with his incomparable sanctity, and reaching from Israel, ultimately to include all peoples. The scandal of the kingdom is that it purports to be the source and the goal of human perception and human action.

The challenge of the kingdom to the modern axiom of relativism is much more profound than the relatively restricted question of eschatology would suggest. There is a single direction mapped by the coordinates of the kingdom: toward the point where God is all in all.[27] The recent fashion of what is called "deconstruction" exemplifies a tendency to dissolve meaning in the claim that there is no overarching pattern in experience, only my response to this or that datum.[28] Deconstructionists are unfairly made responsible for relativism of that sort, since it has long existed under various labels, but deconstruction does make its relativism unmistakable.

Whatever the guise in which relativism might appear, the kingdom of God represents a fundamental alternative. The kingdom's alternative is not to claim that there are absolutes that everyone must recognize (facts or truths or universal laws); that claim of Greek philosophy has long been discredited by the actual disagreements that the statement of any principle (however valid it might have seemed at first) has caused. The alternative of the kingdom as represented in the Psalms is rather that one's subjective experience and one's own actions are part of a pattern of meaning and power that are even now transforming the world.

The world offers no absolutes, because its form is indeed passing away.[29] That change has been taken as a counsel of despair by relativists: meaning is swallowed up by one's passing personal impressions. From the perspective of the kingdom, change is rather the testimony of a dynamism that is restless until it completes its course. There is a force that pushes along the dimensions of time and space, which demands better and purer behavior, as well as our assent to what it does. That is the kingdom along its five coordinates, hopefully celebrated in the book of Psalms.

27. See 1 Cor. 15:28, the close of Paul's explanation of eschatology.
28. See G. Himmelfarb, *On Looking into the Abyss: Untimely Thoughts on Culture and Society* (New York: Knopf, 1994).
29. Again, that is Paul's formulation (see 1 Cor. 7:31).

CHAPTER 3

Jesus' Theology of the Kingdom

Introduction

Five coordinates of the kingdom, then, play a paradigmatic role in the Psalms, and they are the common property of the language of the kingdom in early Judaism. That explains why the kingdom of God is a richly varied concept in early Judaism and why that variety may be measured by reference to the coordinates of language that have been described in the last chapter. A given group would naturally emphasize one coordinate more than the others, but each coordinate would have a place in its vision of the kingdom. Such a commonality of language (in respect of many fundamental concerns) characterizes early Judaism in all its variety within the wider pluralism of the different religious groups of its period.

Jesus and his movement emerged within the setting of early Judaism, so that their vision of the kingdom should also be mapped within the coordinates we have discovered. In principle, any speaker who taught about the kingdom in the milieu of early Judaism may be evaluated by mapping his conception within those coordinates. In this chapter, the purpose is first to explain how Jesus' theology may be known on the basis of the Gospels. On that basis, we will go on to consider what Jesus' general position within the variety of early Judaism must have been. In the next chapter, particular sayings will be analyzed.

The Jesus of Literary History

Not only Jesus' references to the kingdom but also his use of parables to explain what the kingdom means puts him in the company of other Jewish teachers, or rabbis. "Rabbi" means "my master," and is the title most frequently ascribed to Jesus in the Gospels. A rabbi was a local figure, usually *not* a professional teacher, and for that reason the seemingly simple category of "teacher" is not helpful for an assessment of Jesus.

A rabbi was a master in the understanding of what made a given community an instance of Israel, the people of God. Such a rabbi might have disciples who followed his understanding of the correct practice of Israel — including what might be eaten with whom, what made for purity more generally, and how the young should be educated. But he did not need a schoolhouse to be a rabbi. Indeed, in the life of the village, the schoolhouse, the synagogue, and the location where purity was discussed and determined were often one and the same place. The same public site might be where children were taught, where the people met on the Sabbath, and where they would decide whether someone who had been considered unclean should now be included in the common life of the community.

At a later stage, after the destruction of the Temple in 70 CE, a formalization occurred in the rabbinic ethos. The rabbi became the Rabbi, the master of a more specific body of tradition, which became equated in authority with the Torah and associated with an institution, the academy. The first academy is said to have been at Yavneh, near Jerusalem, and to have been founded by Rabbi Yoḥanan ben Zakkai (see Babylonian Talmud *Giṭṭin* 56a, b) toward the end of the Roman siege. The Rabbis after Yavneh did acquire status and wealth that rabbis had not enjoyed before; after all, the destruction of the Temple left them as the most viable principle of authority in Judaism.

Rabbinic Judaism saw a marked emergence of consensus in common loyalty to the Mishnah as of the essence of Torah. The term "mishnah" refers to material that was repeated orally, such as the teachings of a given rabbi. Each rabbi had his distinctive mishnah, much as a professor today will have a distinctive corpus of books to his credit by the end of his career. But by about 200 CE, "the Mishnah" was compiled under the authority of Rabbi Judah, who is known as "the Prince." That Mishnah (always capitalized) established a norm for rabbinic teaching in general. Accordingly, the requirements of what one needed to have studied and mastered in order to be called "Rabbi" were more formal than they had once been. "The Mishnah" emerged out of various *mishnayoth* at the same time that rabbis came to be called "Rabbi," as authorized representatives of a respected institution.

The same Yoḥanan ben Zakkai who was a leader at Yavneh told a parable of the kingdom (Babylonian Talmud *Shabbath* 153a).[1] A king invited his servants to a feast without announcing the hour of the meal. Wise servants attired themselves properly and waited at the door of the king's house. Foolish servants expected definite signs of the meal's preparation and went about their work until they should see those signs. When the king appeared without warning, the wise enjoyed a fine meal, and the foolish servants in their soiled clothing were made to stand and watch.

Jesus is said to have told a similar parable of a feast in order to illustrate the nature of the kingdom (Matt. 22:1-14; Luke 14:16-24). For the moment we can put aside the question whether the historical Jesus directly speaks in the Gospels or the historical Yoḥanan in the Talmud. The fact remains that both speakers are understood *by their own traditions* to have taught concerning the kingdom of God by means of parable. The location of Jesus in early Judaism emerges clearly from a critical reading of the Gospels and Rabbinic literature.[2]

But to characterize Jesus' environment is obviously only one step toward understanding his own distinctive theology. That he had such a theology is evident. His teaching was remembered because it was distinctive. Yet that teaching has been incorporated into Gospels that were produced a generation after his death. Their language is Greek, while his was Aramaic; their cultures are urban and comparatively cosmopolitan (in cities such as Antioch, Damascus, and Rome), while his was rural and comparatively restricted (to villages such as Capernaum and Nazareth). The question of how to infer the historical Jesus from the available sources has produced a literature all its own.[3]

1. For more extensive discussion see B. Chilton and J. I. H. McDonald, *Jesus and the Ethics of the Kingdom* (London: SPCK/Grand Rapids: Eerdmans, 1987) 31-37.

2. I have offered a survey of the Rabbinic corpus in its relevance for the study of the New Testament in "Rabbinic Traditions and Writings," *Dictionary of Jesus and the Gospels*, ed. J. B. Green, S. McKnight, and I. H. Marshall (Downers Grove: InterVarsity, 1992) 651-660.

3. Cf. *Studying the Historical Jesus: Evaluations of the State of Current Research*, ed. B. Chilton and C. A. Evans (New Testament Tools and Studies 19; Leiden: Brill, 1994).

What has emerged after more than a century of intensive study, however, can be stated rather simply. Effectively, the only sources that represent Jesus do so indirectly, as the voices of communities of Christians at a time of great pluralism in the Church, before the creeds established a significant measure of doctrinal agreement. Those communities needed Gospels in order to instruct new converts. As someone approached a primitive community of Jesus' followers out of curiosity about or even enthusiasm for Jesus, that community might naturally be wary in response. After all, churches were under pressure from both civic authorities and synagogue leaders; informers could easily come in the disguise of sympathizers. Before baptism sealed a person as a member of the new movement, as one who might know its other members, its customs, and its lore comprehensively, prospective converts needed to be prepared by a sound catechism that tested their sincerity and commitment over a period of several months. The Synoptic Gospels, those of Matthew, Mark, and Luke, are catechisms produced for that purpose.

Because the first three Gospels emerged from the catechetical work of the movement, when candidates were prepared for baptism, they provide the best indications of the governing concerns of the movement as it initiated new members. The first three Gospels are called "synoptic" because they may be viewed together when they are printed in columns. Unfortunately, their obviously literary relationship has caused scholars to presume that they were composed by scribes working in isolation who copied, one from another.

A comparative approach,[4] served by an understanding of the development of oral traditions into documents in both early Judaism and Christianity, has brought us to the point where deviations of one document from another related document are not assumed to be purely scribal changes. Rather, agreement and disagreement provide opportunities to grasp how one community differed from another in representing Jesus and therefore in ordering its own life. The specific stories told about Jesus and the sayings attributed to him are sometimes the same and sometimes not; that is no surprise, because documents of early Judaism and Rabbinic Judaism also present synoptic relationships in that way. In fact, verbal similarity — agreement word for word in

4. For what follows cf. B. Chilton, *Profiles of a Rabbi: Synoptic Opportunities in Reading about Jesus* (Brown Judaic Studies 177; Atlanta: Scholars, 1989).

comparable material — is often closer in Rabbinic literature than it is in the Gospels. And where the Synoptic Gospels might give us agreement between two or three documents, Rabbinic literature sometimes presents cases of agreement with more than three documents involved.

What *is* notable in the synopticity of the first three Gospels — what distinguishes them from synoptic relations in Rabbinic literature — is the way passages are ordered. It is not just that we can compare individual sayings or stories and their wordings from document to document. That is a standard feature of documents that have a rich history of composition, during which materials were shaped by communities, whether orally or in writing, before they were crystallized in the form of a published writing. In the case of the Synoptic Gospels, we can compare the order in which these materials are presented, one after another, not only the individual passages themselves. That justifies the *literary* characterization of the first three Gospels as the "Synoptics."

Most theories of the relationship among the Synoptic Gospels are unsatisfactory because they fail to account for the differences *and* similarities among them in both wording and order. If one document was simply copied from another, why are words changed, why is material added and subtracted, and why is the order of the first document not followed consistently? But if each Gospel is independent, how do we explain verbatim agreement, the commonly synoptic core of stories and sayings, and their ordering into narratives that largely correspond as they progress?

Once the function of the Synoptic Gospels in the catechesis of the primitive Church is appreciated, the cause of their agreements and their deviations (in all those regards) becomes evident. The first three Gospels reflect the methods of baptismal initiation followed in three influential, nearly contemporaneous, but separate churches.[5] There is a reasonable degree of consensus that Mark was the first of the Gospels to be written, around 71 CE in the environs of Rome. As convention has it, Matthew was subsequently composed, near 80 CE, perhaps in Damascus or elsewhere in Syria, while Luke came later, say in 90 CE, perhaps in Antioch.

At a later stage, a more developed genre of Gospel emerged, in the

---

5. Agreement in order is a measure of a common catechesis; deviations indicate local variation. Contact among the communities may be assumed to have been by both oral and written means, given the evidence regarding communication in early Christianity.

form of discourses of Jesus, built on the Synoptic tradition and supplemented by the oral memory of his teaching. The Gospel according to John is an example of a discursive Gospel, arranged around the themes stated in the prologue (John 1:1-18). It reflects the concerns of the Christian community at Ephesus around 100 CE. The *Gospel according to Thomas* was originally composed around 160 CE as a discursive presentation of answers to questions regarding the best regulation of the community. From its beginnings in Edessa in Syria, *Thomas* later made its way later to Egypt and into the Coptic language (by the fourth century).

The Synoptic Gospels and *Thomas* best present Jesus' teaching concerning the kingdom. (John's Gospel and Paul usually convert the concept of the kingdom into other terms; that change will be discussed below in chapter 6.) We can know of Jesus' own teaching only what we can infer he must have said in order for these sources, the Synoptics and *Thomas* as we can read them today, to have been produced. There is no directly historical information about Jesus, in the sense of a contemporary account written by a person who heard and saw him or a letter dictated by him. We have literary sources from a generation after his death (at the earliest), and they are designed to awaken and inform faith, not to provide historical data.

According to the usual meaning of the word "historical," there is no historical Jesus. But there is a Jesus of literary history: the figure referred to in the Gospels who taught in such a way that a movement began and then flourished to the point that it produced a literature. That Jesus is an inference drawn from the texts as they are read critically. Unless that inference is drawn accurately, it is as impossible to understand the creative contribution of (say) the Roman community reflected in Mark as it is to appreciate Jesus' relationship to contemporary rabbis. Recent inquiry regarding Jesus has been spurred by the desire to understand early Christianity as a religion; unless Jesus is understood, his movement and its development will always be a mystery, to both those in the Church and those outside the Church.

The Jesus of literary history is the rabbi who taught in such a way as to start a movement in early Judaism that later became Christianity. Recovering that Jesus is a matter of exegesis. Exegesis is simply the close reading of a text in order to discover its meaning within its own terms of reference, the cultural context that produced it and that it addressed. The nature of the Gospels requires that we allow for changes in cultural context as one moves from Jesus' original circle, through the circles of disciples after his death, who framed much of the material in the Gospels in order to teach others, and on to the Gospels, which were composed in Hellenistic cities.

An exegesis of the Gospels must be a generative exegesis. We need to trace how things Jesus did and said generated a movement and produced a memory. That movement and memory then generated successive phases, each with its own social context, until the time the Gospels were written.[6] After that time, of course, the generation of fresh meanings in new contexts continued: each age has appropriated a distinct portrait of Jesus.[7] To identify what is new in each portrait is fairly straightforward, when we know what picture of Jesus was current when the new portrait was offered and when we can say what people at the time of the portrait thought about Jesus. In the case of the Gospels, we are left to infer the portraits that have been overlaid during the time the Gospels took shape. And (above all) we are left to infer the portrait that generated the others — that is, the Jesus of literary history.

Scholarship of the New Testament usually works backward: from the texts we read to the Jesus that we need to infer. Reflection backward is sensible because we need to let the evidence (the texts) control our inferences (the Jesus of literary history) rather than the reverse. But a scholar can do what most readers cannot be expected to do. A scholar will constantly have in mind the Jesus that she or he is constructing when a given saying is analyzed as the product of a later stage of the movement rather than as Jesus' own. There is a constant cross-checking in the history of exegesis to see how one's vision of the theology of the primitive communities impinges on one's vision of Jesus, and vice versa.

Sometimes the decision might be that a saying is essentially formed by a community in Jesus' name, sometimes that it has been significantly changed during the course of transmission. But the point is that, as soon as such a decision is made, one's picture of Jesus changes. As a scholar proceeds, the balance between Jesus as the initiator of the movement

---

6. A technical account of generative exegesis is offered in B. Chilton, *A Feast of Meanings: Eucharistic Theologies from Jesus through Johannine Circles* (Supplements to *Novum Testamentum* 72; Leiden: Brill, 1994) 146-158.

7. See D. C. Duling, *Jesus Christ through History* (New York: Harcourt Brace Jovanovich, 1979).

and Jesus as the product of the movement changes. But we cannot speak of Jesus at all unless we appreciate that certain sayings represent the generative point of the tradition that developed in his name.

In the next chapter, I will specify those sayings concerning the kingdom that represent that generative point: the kingdom of God in Jesus' theology may be inferred on the basis of the Synoptic Gospels and *Thomas*. The development of his theology into other theologies will be treated in chapter 6. Of course, I have identified the generative sayings only by tracing back from the texts as they are to Jesus as he must have been within Judaism.[8] Those who wish to test my results will need to put the discussion in chapter 4 together with the discussion in chapter 6, in order to see the history of the tradition as I understand it. Jesus can only be understood *after* the history of the tradition has been analyzed and the generative core placed in its appropriate context. The discussion here and in the next chapter presupposes that scholarly procedure, but it will begin from the generative core, which offers insight into the Jesus of literary history.

Considerable controversy has surrounded the recent publication of the initial results of the "Jesus Seminar."[9] Some readers have been offended at the idea of scholars sitting around a table and voting on which of Jesus' sayings should be accepted as authentic. Yet the Seminar simply did in public, and commonly, what scholars have been doing for the better part of two hundred years. Until the recent impetus to infer the Jesus of literary history, it had even been a commonplace of education in seminaries to say that Jesus could not be known at all in historical terms since the Gospels reflect communities of faith rather than attempts to keep records.[10] Somehow most preachers neglected to say that from the pulpit, despite their years of training. The Jesus Seminar has pressed both scholars and pastors into the open, and resistance is only natural.

Public discourse has proceeded as if Christian theologians accepted the Gospels as literal history, and those same theologians have

8. For a full and technical deployment of the method, see B. Chilton, *God in Strength: Jesus' Announcement of the Kingdom* (Studien zum Neuen Testament und seiner Umwelt 1; Freistadt: Plöchl, 1979; reprinted in The Biblical Seminar series, Sheffield: JSOT, 1987).

9. R. W. Funk, R. W. Hoover, and the Jesus Seminar, *The Five Gospels: The Search for the Authentic Words of Jesus* (New York: Macmillan, 1993).

10. That was the position taken most famously by Rudolf Bultmann; see his *New Testament and Mythology*, ed. and tr. S. M. Ogden (London: SCM, 1985).

avoided offending believers with their skepticism. So believers are increasingly persuaded that they must be uncritical in order to believe, and critical skeptics conclude that all forms of faith are credulous. Each side has encouraged the other to make religion into a reaction against reasoned reflection. This is a principal reason that American discourse concerning religion is ill-informed, a dangerous situation in a country in which different religious communities live side by side. Instead of dialogue, special interests for given points of view insist that theirs is the only way; there are orthodoxies of fundamentalists, orthodoxies of Catholics, orthodoxies of Islam, orthodoxies of Jungians, orthodoxies of professing atheists, and more. Unless and until the grounds of such perspectives are appreciated, the only contact these communities will have with one another will be in the form of conflict. Theologians, believers, and nonbelieving observers of religion must all at least understand what is involved in faith, if religious tolerance is to be preserved and enhanced.

But if the publicity of the Jesus Seminar provided a service, its results cannot be taken as representative of the discipline of biblical criticism or as authoritative in any sense. Scholars in the Seminar disagreed in their voting, the membership changed from meeting to meeting, and most of those who took part tended to deny the historical worth of the Gospels from the outset. The sayings presented in this book as generative were all seriously considered by the seminar, and the published results of that discussion are nearly always interesting and informative. But I have made my own decisions and followed my own judgment in authenticating the Jesus of literary history within the larger body of material that reflects the diverse faith of primitive Christians. Those followers of Jesus, of course, had their own understandings of authenticity, which encouraged them to interpret Jesus' teaching actively within the context of their own experience. Their interpretation of Jesus' theology of the kingdom will be discussed in chapter 6.

Jesus' Map of the Kingdom

The coordinates of the kingdom as understood by Jesus are those of early Judaism. He had a view of God as king, a vision of his divine activity, that involved its eschatology, its transcendence, its ethics, its purity, and its radiance. In a general sense, Jesus' vision may simply be said to be that of early Judaism, but the level of generality involved makes that statement seem banal.

After all, early Judaic conceptions of God as king were richly varied.[11] Was Jesus' viewpoint as apocalyptic as the Essenes', or was it more in the nature of the activism of those who took up arms against Rome? Did he accept or challenge Sadducean notions of the Temple as the seat of God's royal power on earth? Did he agree with the Pharisees that purity was a necessary condition of the kingdom; and if so, what definition of purity did he embrace? How far would Jesus have gone in approving the correlation of the kingdom with divine Wisdom as that was worked out in characteristic sources of Hellenistic Judaism?

In the past, even the recent past, scholars have too quickly embraced one conception of the kingdom in early Judaism as the starting point for understanding Jesus without considering the others. Schweitzer and, more recently, E. P. Sanders[12] correctly identified an apocalyptic stream of thought during the first century and then located Jesus within it. But what of Jesus' relation to other streams of thought? Similarly, S. G. F. Brandon[13] looked only to the history of revolutionary movements in the first century as the context of Jesus' kingdom. Extreme selectivity in comparison (together with obvious anachronism) permits Barbara Thiering[14] to picture Jesus as a renegade Essene who resisted the "Teacher of Righteousness" (John the Baptist, she claims), just as it permits Harvey Falk[15] to portray Jesus as a Pharisee who wished to proselytize non-Jews. John Dominic Crossan, meanwhile, blandly remarks that "Hellenistic Judaism" was the only Judaism of the period, and so makes his Jesus in the mold of a roving philosopher.[16]

---

11. See the discussion in the closing section of chapter 2 above, "Visions of the Kingdom," pp. 42-44.

12. See *Jesus and Judaism* (Philadelphia: Fortress, 1985).

13. See *Jesus and the Zealots: A Study of the Political Factor in Primitive Christianity* (Manchester: Manchester University, 1967).

14. See *Jesus and the Riddle of the Dead Sea Scrolls: Unlocking the Secrets of His Life Story* (San Francisco: Harper, 1993). Other arguments she makes on the basis of alleged connections with the Scrolls are not tenable; her speculations in regard to Jesus' sexual activities are a case in point.

15. See *Jesus the Pharisee: A New Look at the Jewishness of Jesus* (New York: Paulist, 1985).

16. *The Historical Jesus: The Life of a Mediterranean Jewish Peasant* (San Francisco: Harper/Edinburgh: Clark, 1991) 418. For a fuller discussion of the entire question, see

Not all such reconstructions are of equal merit. (Schweitzer's, Sanders's, Brandon's, and Crossan's have rightly received close attention; Falk's and Thiering's have not.) There is something to be learned from each, perhaps about the history of the period or the interpretation of particular texts. But the glaring fault of them all is their lack of an overall perspective of variety in early Judaism.

The starting point in understanding Jesus must not be that we know what sort of Jew he was. That is precisely the information we do not have.[17] Rather, critical reflection needs to begin with an appreciation of how the kingdom was spoken of in early Judaism (as above in chapter 2) and then proceed to map Jesus' vision of the kingdom within the coordinates of that language (as below in chapter 4). Comparison with varieties of Judaism can be pursued on that basis, just as the development of Jesus' message among his followers can be traced. The generative exegesis of Jesus' teaching permits us, in short, to locate Jesus in Judaism, just as it helps us to appreciate the emergence and development of earliest Christianity. Above all, generative exegesis avoids the easy fallacy of equating Jesus with the sort of Judaism or Christianity that happens to appeal to us.

B. Chilton, "Jesus within Judaism," in *Judaism in Late Antiquity.* II: *Historical Syntheses,* ed. J. Neusner (Handbuch der Orientalistik 17; Leiden: Brill, 1994) 262-284.

17. The supposition that Jesus is essentially a figure of Rabbinic Judaism is an obvious anachronism, since Rabbinic Judaism (as distinct from early Judaism) did not emerge until well after Jesus' death. For that reason, the approach of Geza Vermes is simply uncritical; see his *The Religion of Jesus the Jew* (Minneapolis: Fortress, 1993).

CHAPTER 4

Jesus' Theology of the Kingdom

Exegetical

When people used the phrase "kingdom of God" in early Judaism, they were striving to understand how God relates to his world. Use of the phrase both reflected and encouraged a vivid attempt to conceive of God's vindication of his people. What would he do? When would he act? To the benefit of precisely which people? How would we know how to cooperative with God's rule? One addressed such inevitable questions in speaking of God as king, even as one envisaged God fully in command of all the circumstances and vicissitudes that his people might confront. The concept referred to that commanding and all-consuming divine activity and was articulated to cope with the questions inherent in the very notion that God is king. Variety among differing conceptions was prevalent, but there was a consistency in the dimensions within which the kingdom could be described. God's rule would be along the coordinates of eschatology, transcendence, judgment, purity, and radiance (as discussed in chapter 2).

Jesus' particular theology of the kingdom is accessible by means of an exegesis of the sayings attributed to him that most directly attest his own concerns within the context of the early Judaism of his time (as discussed in chapter 3). We take up just those sayings here, in chapter 4, and then relate his theology to his characteristic activities in chapter 5. How that material fed the generation of distinctive theologies in the early church, theologies that have influenced the presentation of Jesus' sayings in the Gospels themselves, will take up our attention in chapter 6.

The Eschatological Coordinate

The most basic understanding of the kingdom that a rabbi wished to convey would naturally be the conception that he urged his disciples to repeat most frequently. Many rabbis are represented in the literature of Judaism as leaving behind no specific recommendation for prayer. That, of course, is not the situation in the case of Jesus. In addition to providing advice concerning prayer that involves the kingdom, Jesus also entrusted his followers with a model of announcing the kingdom, as well as with an esoteric assurance of the kingdom. All three sayings manifest a concern primarily with the eschatological coordinate of the kingdom.

"Your Kingdom Come"

Of the two versions of the Lord's Prayer in the New Testament (Matt. 6:9-15; Luke 11:2-4), Luke's is widely considered the earlier in form. Matthew presents what is, in effect, a commentary woven together with the prayer:

Matthew	Luke
Our father in heaven	Father,
let your name be sanctified;	let your name be sanctified;
your kingdom come,	your kingdom come!
your will be done	
on earth as in heaven!	
Our daily bread	Our daily bread
give us today;	give us each day;
and forgive us our debts,	and forgive us our sins,
as we also	for we ourselves also
have forgiven our debtors;	forgive our every debtor;
and lead us not	and lead us not

into temptation,
but deliver us from the
evil one.

into temptation.

Certain uniquely Matthean elements appear to be expansions on the model. "Your will be done" explicates "your kingdom come." The late Philip Sigal identified texts of rabbinic prayers that present a similar focus on the will of God;[1] as a gloss in the Lord's Prayer, the phrase "your will be done" would be quite early, but not at the generative point of the prayer. God's "kingdom" was Jesus' focus. The reference to God's "will" was an attempt to explain the meaning of the kingdom within a community no longer directly in contact with the ethos and teaching of Jesus.

The distinctiveness of the Lord's Prayer in Matthew as compared to Luke should make it plain beyond a doubt that one Gospel cannot be explained simply on the basis of one scribe copying from another. Matthew gives us the version of the prayer used in Damascus (ca. 80 CE), just as Luke provides us with the version used in Antioch (ca. 90 CE). Both might have kept the silence of Mark, where no version of the prayer is presented. In Mark's Rome (ca. 71 CE) the prayer was apparently taught outside the context of the initial catechesis, perhaps in private oral instruction.

Had Matthew and Luke followed the Markan policy, the version of the prayer in *Didache* 8, which is comparable to Matthew's, would have been our only literary source of the Lord's Prayer from documents of primitive Christianity.[2] According to the *Didache* the prayer

---

1. "Early Christian and Rabbinic Liturgical Affinities: Exploring Liturgical Acculturation," *New Testament Studies* 30 (1984) 63-90, here 74; see Mishnah *Aboth* 2:4; Babylonian Talmud *Berakhoth* 29b, 38a; *Yoma* 53b; *Megillah* 27b. One analogy (in Jerusalem Talmud *Berakhoth* 7d) is even linked to a request "to vanquish and remove from our hearts the inclination to do evil."

2. The *Didache* is a brief catechism designed to introduce the faith to non-Jews who already have some familiarity with both Judaism and Christianity. The document probably comes from early in the second century; see Kirsopp Lake, *The Apostolic Fathers* I (Loeb Classical Library; New York: Putnam, 1912). The Lord's Prayer in Matthew is the evident basis of the version in the *Didache,* which is elaborated in the interest of liturgy. The relationship between Matthew and the *Didache* supports the inferences that both documents originated in Syria and that Matthew was earlier. For recent discussion of the *Didache* see Robert A. Kraft, "Didache," *The Anchor Bible Dictionary* II, ed. D. N. Freedman (New York: Doubleday, 1992) 197-198.

is to be said thrice daily, as is the *'Amidah* in Judaism. An increasingly liturgical portrayal of the prayer, from Luke through Matthew and on to the *Didache,* is obvious. In some ways, it is the *Didache's* version, with its concluding doxology ("for yours is the power and glory, forever and ever") that is most like the later practice of traditional Christianity.

The relative sparseness of Luke's version has won it virtually unanimous recognition among scholars as the nearest to the form of an outline that Jesus would have recommended. In view of the tendency we have seen toward an increasingly liturgical presentation (a filling out of the model), that verdict seems correct. Accordingly, the generative model of the Lord's Prayer consists of calling God father, confessing that his name should be sanctified and that his kingdom should come, and then asking for daily bread, forgiveness, and not to be lead into temptation. (The meaning of the last request has caused great confusion, although the issue is not directly pertinent to the topic of this chapter. For the original sense, see Appendix B, "Jesus' Prayer and the War of Worlds.") Because a model is at issue, rather than a liturgy, attempts to fix a precise form of words simply exceed the bounds of any achievable certainty.

Luke 11:2b-4 functions as a paradigm in its brevity, and its terse petitions for elemental needs — bread, pardon, integrity — appear nearly anticlimactic in comparison with the sorts of appeals that were possible in the early Judaism of the period. The Lukan context (11:1-2a, 5-13) presents the prayer in a didactic manner, as something to be learned in contrast to other formulations. The Matthean context is more liturgical, invoking as it does the issues of almsgiving (6:2-4), inappropriate and appropriate places of prayer (vv. 5-6), putting prayer into words (vv. 7-8), and fasting (vv. 16-17).[3]

The generative model permits us to place the elements in the recommended outline of prayer under two major headings:

> *address* of God (1) as father, (2) with sanctification of God's name
> and (3) vigorous assent to the coming of God's kingdom, and
> *petition* for (1) bread, (2) forgiveness, and (3) constancy.

---

3. The issue of fasting is the context preceding (rather than following) the Lord's Prayer in *Didache* 8.

The two major headings are clearly distinguished in grammatical terms. God is addressed in the third person, as father, and this is followed by imperatives in the third person ("let your name be sanctified, "your kingdom come") while the plea for bread is in the imperative of the second person ("give us"), as are the appeals for forgiveness ("forgive us") and constancy ("lead us not").

There is a symmetry between the two major divisions of the prayer, such that God's fatherhood is linked to the request for bread, the sanctification of his name is related to forgiveness, and the plea for constancy is tied to the kingdom. By means of the language associated with the kingdom and its structural link to the theme of constancy ("lead us not into temptation"), the prayer provides a clear indication of the eschatological coordinate of Jesus' thought.

That the kingdom is to "come" (from *erchomai* in Greek, *'ata'* in Aramaic) provides us with an index of distinctively eschatological thinking. The verb is not usually associated with the kingdom in Judaic literature, where it is more natural to speak of when the kingdom is to be "revealed." Speaking of it as to "come" is obviously a matter of anticipating the future, and to that extent it is surprising that there has been any doubt that Jesus' thinking was eschatological. But the type of eschatology at issue is striking. What is prayed for might come sooner or later or not at all; as an object of prayer, the kingdom cannot be conceived of as coming at a fixed point in time. In that sense, it is eschatological, but not apocalyptic. For that reason, the link of the acceptance of the kingdom in the address of God with the petition not to be led into temptation in the second part of the prayer is logical and appropriate. The time of the kingdom is sufficiently indeterminate to demand the grace of a constant integrity; at the end of the prayer one must pray for the assurance that one will be able to pray again another day.

"The Kingdom of God Has Come Near"

Reference to the kingdom as "arriving" or "coming near" was characteristic of Jesus' usage. The fundamental metaphor involves physical movement from one location to another. Conceived of as that which is to come, the kingdom is also inevitably conceived of as in some sense occupying space; only that which already exists tangibly can arrive. That which is to come takes up a certain volume of space and displaces other things both in its arrival and in the process of arriving. Jesus' eschatological language exploits that spatial implication of a future hope.

A typical example of his preaching of the kingdom's arrival appears in the same source, common to Matthew and Luke, which also provides us with the versions of the Lord's Prayer that we have already considered. This source is known as "Q" among scholars and was a collection of Jesus' sayings comparable in some ways to the mishnah a rabbi might provide his disciples to learn. In its earliest phase, "Q" was most likely oral, although it went through further phases before its material was available to the writers of the Gospels of Matthew and Luke. Differences between Matthew and Luke in material that derives from this source (differences such as the Lord's Prayer illustrates) show that "Q" was not a stable written source but a collection of Jesus' teachings that went through local variations as it was transmitted. As an Aramaic collection, "Q" probably originated around 35 CE among the twelve disciples, whose communal activity was centered in Jerusalem.

Along with the Lord's Prayer, "Q" provides us with Jesus' commission of a select group of followers to preach and act in his name (see Matt. 10:5-15; Luke 9:1-6). These twelve disciples are Jesus' representatives, and the teaching that they are to convey is the signature concern of "Q." Matthew gives the precise form of words involved: the kingdom of God that is to be proclaimed "has come near" (Matt. 10:7).[4] The term is used quite precisely, a form of the verb "come near" (Greek *engizō*), but in the perfect tense. In that tense "come near" must refer to that which is so near that its approach has been completed, although it is not yet completely present. The form of the verb represents the cusp between the process of arriving and arrival itself.

"Has come near" is thus used to convey a precise meaning, and it represents a verb in Aramaic *(qereb)* that is used of eschatological realities just as they are about to impinge on the world as we know it. In the book of Daniel, for example, the son of man — an angelic figure — is said to be presented before God; at the climactic moment, he is "made

---

4. Luke 9:2 makes a summary reference, simply to preaching the kingdom of God. The locution "kingdom of the heavens" is a development of language in Matthew that reflects later usage in Judaism (see chapter 6).

to come near" (a form of *qereb*) to God by the heavenly court (Dan. 7:13). Jesus' usage conceives of a similar movement, but from heaven to earth. The kingdom of God, which already exists in the rule of the heavenly court, has come so near to our experience as to impinge upon it. That is why praying for the kingdom makes sense and why announcing it (in the appropriate terms) is a pressing task of the disciples.

The heavenly aspect of the kingdom is frequently missed by interpreters, who sometimes imagine that eschatology excludes the present reality of what is anticipated. The contrary is the case. In the example cited from the book of Daniel, the "son of man" in chapter 7 is the angel of Israel; the seer pictures him as presented before God (7:13) in anticipation of that time when Israel on the ground would be vindicated over its enemies (v. 18). The vision in heaven confirms the expectation of what is to occur on the earth. Jesus' focus was more on the kingdom than on the son of man,[5] but his conviction that what he anticipated already existed was no less firm than what the book of Daniel reflects.

"Those Who Will Not Taste Death until They See the Kingdom"

The heavenly reality of the kingdom is the key to what is otherwise one of the most mysterious of Jesus' sayings. It is preserved not in "Q" but in the source common to all three Synoptic Gospels. The discussion of that source will concern us in a moment; the saying itself demands immediate attention (Matt. 16:28; Mark 9:1; Luke 9:27):[6]

> There are some here of those standing,
> who will not taste death
> until they see the kingdom of God.

5. Of course he taught concerning that figure as well, but that is not the present concern. See B. Chilton, "The Son of Man: Human and Heavenly," in *The Four Gospels: 1992*, ed. F. van Segbroeck, C. M. Tuckett, G. van Belle, J. Verheyden (Festschrift for Frans Neirynck; BETL 100; Leuven, 1992) 203-218, also published in *Approaches to Ancient Judaism: Religious and Theological Studies,* ed. J. Neusner (South Florida Studies in the History of Judaism 81; Atlanta: Scholars, 1993) 97-114.

6. The wording of the saying in each Gospel is distinct; the form cited here is what probably generated those distinct (but obviously related) versions.

Of all of Jesus' sayings concerning the kingdom of God, this has been the least understood.

The typical understanding is that the saying is a promise to Jesus' followers that they will not die before the kingdom arrives. That involves an eschatological (indeed, apocalyptic) view of the kingdom in Jesus' teaching. If that meaning is accepted, the promise attributed to Jesus was evidently false. What should we make of that error? The obvious alternatives are either that Jesus was badly mistaken or that his followers were badly mistaken in attributing the promise to him. The first alternative involves accepting that Jesus set a fixed time for the coming of the kingdom.[7] The second involves denying that he ever said what the Synoptics said he said.[8] Both alternatives are defensible on the basis of the Greek text of the Gospels. Both can offer an explanation of how the saying came to be shaped as it has been. On the first view, the promise (however embarrassing in the light of subsequent events) was preserved because Jesus said it. On the second view, the promise was promulgated as a result of the apocalyptic fervor of later Christians who attributed to Jesus predictive powers that he did not personally claim to have.

There were Greek-speaking Christians of the first century who believed that the kingdom would come before they died. Paul even speaks — with withering sarcasm — of those who believed they already were reigning in the kingdom (1 Cor. 4:8). Such Christians would obviously have understood Jesus' saying in the way modern interpreters have. But when the saying is approached through the lens of Judaic conceptions and the Aramaic language, its meaning appears quite different. In this case, as in others, placing a saying within its generative context both reveals its initial meaning and explains how other meanings were attributed to it.

Even as the saying stands, it is apparent that its meaning is not literal. No scholar would seriously argue that Jesus is promising that the kingdom will come and that then his followers will die. Two things about the saying, which relate to one another in order to convey its particular meaning, have confused interpreters. The first is that "those who will not taste death" has a particular meaning in its originating context. The second is that the form of the promise is not a prediction of death.

---

7. So, in the manner of Schweitzer, E. P. Sanders, *Jesus and Judaism* (London: SCM, 1985) 142-146.

8. So, most recently, Marcus Borg, *Jesus in Contemporary Scholarship* (Valley Forge: Trinity Press International, 1994) 54, 86-87.

The phrase "those who will not taste death" refers in Judaism to people who *never* die. In the Bible such immortals include Enoch, who walked with God and disappeared (Gen. 5:24), and Elijah, who was taken up in a whirlwind into heaven (2 Kgs. 2:11). By the time of Jesus, that the place of Moses' grave was unknown was taken to mean that he, too, was among those who were never to taste death.[9] There was also an expectation in some circles that the messiah was to appear with companions who had not tasted death (see 4 Ezra 6:25, 26).

Looked at through the lens of early Judaic expectations, then, the saying refers to figures who never die. But if so, why does it next say that they will not taste death *until* the kingdom comes? Although the literal sense of the grammar seems ridiculous, the question remains: how does the wording avoid implying that those who are deathless will die when God's rule arrives? The problem of the literal grammar seems to remain, even if the meaning of "those who will not taste death" is better understood.

Semitic grammar, however, helps us to see the real meaning of the statement. In a recent study, I built on the work of Klaus Beyer in order to show that the form of speech "*x* will not happen until *y*" is used in Hebrew and Aramaic in order to insist that *both parts of the statement are valid.* The plainest example is in the book of Genesis (28:15), when God promises Jacob: "I will not depart from you until I have done that of which I have spoken to you." Anyone who is interested in more instances need only consult the technical literature;[10] the point that is illustrated again and again is that statements of that kind are deliberately emphatic assertions. In our example God is saying "I will never leave you *and* I will do what I promised."

Literal grammar would make God a charlatan in Genesis. He would

---

9. See Josephus, *Jewish Antiquities* 4.325, where Moses takes his leave of Eleazar and Joshua when a cloud suddenly arrives and he disappears. Moses and Enoch are popularly associated as both "departing into the divine" in *Antiquities* 1.85 and 3.96, but Josephus himself prefers to use the language of disappearance in regard to Moses. He uses the same language to describe Elijah's end in *Antiquities* 9.28. For further considerations, see B. Chilton, "The Transfiguration: Dominical Assurance and Apostolic Vision," *New Testament Studies* 27 (1980) 115-124. Substantially the same argument is made in Augustín Del Agua, "The Narrative of the Transfiguration as a Derashic Scenification of a Faith Confession (Mark 9.2-8 Par.)," *New Testament Studies* 39 (1993) 340-354.

10. See B. Chilton, *A Feast of Meanings: Eucharistic Theologies from Jesus through Johannine Circles* (Supplements to *Novum Testamentum* 72; Leiden: Brill, 1994) 169-171.

be telling Jacob that he would merely fulfill the letter of his commitments, and then desert Jacob. Such a reading undermines a major theme of the entire book of Genesis. Similarly, it undermines the sense of Jesus' assertion to imagine the deathless figures expiring once the kingdom of God is realized. The point is rather that the immortals never die, and that the coming of the kingdom is as certain as their immortality.

This reading of Jesus' promise concerning those who will never taste death, interpreted from the point of view of the language of early Judaism, is confirmed by the passage that follows, the Transfiguration (Matt. 17:1-9; Mark 9:2-10; Luke 9:28-36). There, Jesus actually appears with Moses and Elijah, two of those who were said never to have tasted death. The story of the Transfiguration is a visionary representation of Jesus' promise. Jesus had insisted that the kingdom's coming was as certain as the immortality of figures such as Moses and Elijah, and three of his disciples — Peter, James, and John — attest to the truth of his assurance with their vision of Moses and Elijah with Jesus. The type of assurance represented by such a vision can be compared to the Hymns of Qumran (the *Hodayoth*), in which members of the community celebrated the presence of angels already in their midst, who were to be with them in the final war against the sons of darkness.[11]

Of course, the saying in its own context is of a different tenor from the prayer for the kingdom and the announcement of the kingdom. It is less a public statement than a proclamation for insiders, a vivid recollection of the basic, inner truth of their life together. The saying in fact comes to us from a select, inner circle of Jesus' followers (Peter, James, and John) in which the leading person was Peter. Peter delivered his gospel to Paul during a period of fifteen days around the year 35 CE (see Gal. 1:18); by that time (which was also the time of "Q" in an early phase) a Petrine source obviously existed.[12] That is the source that provides us with Jesus' assurance that the kingdom that is to come already exists, and exists with the certainty of its heavenly witnesses.

---

11. 1QH 6:10-14, in the midst of which comes the statement, "All them that follow Thy counsel hast thou brought into communion with Thee, and hast given them common state with the Angels of Thy Presence." See Theodor H. Gaster, *The Dead Sea Scriptures* (Garden City: Doubleday, 1976).

12. In all probability, it was an oral source (like "Q" in its Aramaic phase), although it was made public by Peter and his circle. In that sense the source was oral, but also published.

Summary

Prayer that the kingdom of God should come clearly marks out the kingdom as that which might encounter us in the future. In that sense, especially because Jesus provided a form of prayer for general use that includes a petition for the kingdom's coming, the eschatological coordinate of the kingdom is evident and prominent. At the same time, there is marked and deliberate uncertainty in regard to the time of the kingdom, a reluctance to embrace the precise anticipations of apocalyptic literature. That uncertainty in regard to timing is balanced with an assurance of the actual, present reality of the kingdom in heaven. It is announced as so near as effectively to have finished its movement toward us and as being as reliable as the immortal prophets in the heavenly court. "Q" provides us with the more general statements of the eschatological kingdom, while the Petrine source conveys Jesus' esoteric assurance to his followers of the kingdom's reality.

The Transcendent Coordinate

Transcendence is a concept that is often misunderstood in modern discussion. Because it refers properly to what is beyond the terms of reference of our world, the assumption is sometimes made that transcendence must refer to a timeless realm of ideas, as in Platonic thought. Any such assumption is misleading, in regard to both Plato and the book of Psalms. Plato's ideal forms were meant to explain how the realm of intellect was *linked* to the realm of perception, not to separate the two.[13] And we have already seen (in chapter 2) that the book of Psalms understands God's kingship as local in Zion, so that one day his rule might surpass every boundary in its fullness. The point is not the timelessness of certain ideas but the dynamic force of a rule that already is exerted in the Temple and whose natural horizon is the whole of cre-

---

13. The reasoning is that "the world has been framed in the likeness of that which is apprehended by reason and mind and is unchangeable, and must therefore of necessity, if this be admitted, be a copy of something." See *Timaeus* 28, here in the translation of B. Jowett, *The Dialogues of Plato* II (New York: Random House, 1937).

ation. That biblical, dynamic transcendence, not Platonic idealism, is what is at issue in Jesus' teaching.[14]

"If I by the Spirit of God Cast Out Demons . . ."

The dynamic quality of transcendence in Jesus' teaching is evident in a famous saying from "Q" (Matt. 12:28; Luke 11:20):

> If I by the spirit of God cast out demons,
> then the kingdom of God has arrived upon you.

Luke's version of the saying prefers "finger of God" to "spirit of God"; the change both alludes back to the "finger of God" by which Moses worked wonders in Egypt (Exod. 8:19) and avoids equating the power of exorcism with the spirit of God in baptism. In this case Matthew gives the more accurate version of "Q," but the meaning is evident in both Gospels. Jesus saw the removal of unclean spirits in response to his activity as a clear indication that God's kingdom had arrived or come (*phthanō* in Greek, *meṭa'* in Aramaic) on those who witnessed his activity.

That Jesus insists here that the kingdom has actually arrived, while his proclamation refers to the kingdom's nearness, has understandably caused confusion. Some scholars (following Schweitzer) have seen the arrival only as nearness, while others (following Dodd) have seen nearness only in arrival. Complicated interpretations and arguments over translation have been the predictable result of tension between the two camps. The dispute between partisans of "consistent eschatology" and partisans of "realized eschatology" has sometimes seemed more dogmatic than exegetical, as has been discussed in chapter 1. The best example is perhaps Dodd's insistence that "has come near" *(engiken)* be translated "has come" in the *New English Bible*.[15] His argument was that Jesus can have intended only one meaning both in the public announce-

14. The influence of Platonic thought *is* evident in the later literature of Wisdom, especially Wisdom of Solomon 7. See R. B. Y. Scott, *The Way of Wisdom in the Old Testament* (New York: Macmillan, 1971) 212-222.

15. See his article "The Kingdom of God Has Come," *Expository Times* 48 (1936-37) 138-142. The issue is discussed in B. Chilton, *God in Strength: Jesus' Announcement of the Kingdom* (Studien zum Neuen Testament und seiner Umwelt 1; Freistadt: Plöchl, 1979; reprinted in The Biblical Seminar series, Sheffield: JSOT, 1987) 56-57.

ment of the kingdom and in his explanation of his exorcisms and that the actual rendering of words in Greek should be adjusted to suit that meaning. When great scholars resort to such desperate arguments, we should suspect that the terms in which the debate concerning the kingdom have evolved are not conducive to a clear apprehension of Jesus' message within its own context.

One advantage of seeing the distinct coordinates of the kingdom in Jesus' theology is that we can easily explain why in one aspect (eschatology) the kingdom is near, while in another aspect (transcendence) the kingdom has arrived. That arrival is limited, and so there is no question of all the eschatological promises being realized in the present. But to qualify the arrival of the kingdom as limited in no sense denies the reality of God's rule. After all, even an eschatological hope conceives of what is to come as already existent in heaven. And Jesus' saying about the kingdom and his exorcisms maintains that the kingdom is not only real, but a matter of what occurs in the experience of his hearers. Along its transcendent coordinate, the kingdom arrives in a local, sporadic, but intense occurrence, so as to clear away demons. The removal of their influence makes a place that is to be like every place, because it is where God rules.

Because Jesus' own activity is the particular occasion of the kingdom here ("If *I* by the spirit of God . . ."), an implicit christology is involved. The unspoken assertion is that his exorcisms are effective of the kingdom in a way that others' are not. The link between Jesus and the kingdom becomes explicit in a saying from the *Gospel according to Thomas* (saying 82):[16]

> Whoever is near me is near the fire,
> and whoever is far from me is far from the kingdom.

The imagery of fire is prominent in Jesus' teaching (in this case see Luke 12:49) and serves to evoke the connection in his mind between the local, dynamic incursion of the kingdom (the fire) and the permanence of God's triumph (the kingdom itself).

---

16. An edition and translation that is widely available and useful is Marvin Meyer's *The Gospel of Thomas: The Hidden Sayings of Jesus* (San Francisco: Harper, 1992). By contrast, Harold Bloom's alleged "Reading" (in what amounts to a postscript in Meyer's book) is nothing more than special pleading for the pseudo-Gnostic christology that many books from Harper indulge in lately.

Allowance must be made in *Thomas*, just as in the canonical Gospels, for the influence of later theologies on the text as it stands. The origin of *Thomas*'s tradition is a collection of Jesus' sayings gathered after his resurrection by a disciple called Judah (Judas in its Hellenized form), to whom Jesus gave the name "the twin" (*Toma'* in Aramaic, "Thomas" in its Hellenized form). Jesus gave nicknames to several of his disciples; that is why Simon comes to be known as "the rock" (Matt. 16:18: "Petros" in Greek, "Kepha'" in Aramaic)[17] and James and John are called "thunder-brothers" (Mark 3:17: "Boanerges").[18]

The famous incident of Thomas's doubt of Jesus' resurrection in John 20:24-29 shows that at the time John was written (around 100 CE in Ephesus) its community was aware of a tradition of dialogue between Thomas and the risen Jesus. That tradition was later developed, with much borrowing from the canonical Gospels, and recorded in Edessa near 160 CE. The ascetic emphasis of Christianity in Edessa was a profound influence on *Thomas;* a central saying (saying 22), for example, stipulates that one must be neither male nor female in order to enter the kingdom. A denial of sexuality is manifest. The ascetic version of *Thomas* was then expanded in Egypt under the influence of Gnosticism and rendered into Coptic by the fourth century. By that stage, even the prophets of Israel could be dismissed as voices of "the dead" (saying 52): such a denigration of the Hebrew Scriptures was routine among many Gnostic groups.

Even after one has allowed for the influences of Egyptian Gnosticism and Syrian asceticism, there is a further complication in assessing the sayings of *Thomas* as statements of Jesus during the period of his public activity. *Thomas* conveys what it explicitly calls sayings of the risen Jesus (or "living Jesus," as the first statement in the document calls him): the generative point of the tradition is Jesus' encounter with Judas Thomas after the resurrection. That encounter was portrayed as consistent with Jesus' teaching before he was crucified, since the identity of Jesus before and after the resurrection was a principal claim inherent within the faith. But *Thomas* does not set itself up in relation to the sources of the historical Jesus in the way that the Synoptic Gospels do.

The reference to the fire and the kingdom in saying 82 is not

---

17. See John 1:42; 1 Cor. 1:12; 3:22; 9:5; 15:5; Gal. 1:18; 2:9, 11, 14. The form "Cephas" is a distortion that comes through the Greek and Latin transliterations.

18. The Aramaic form is simply transliterated in Mark, and then translated.

inherently ascetic or Gnostic, but it could be explained as an example of how Jesus was understood to speak by those who experienced him as risen from the dead. After all, he had said "Everyone will be salted with fire" (Mark 9:49); saying 82 might be seen as a further application of the imagery of fire in the context of the resurrection. At the same time, in its implicit christology, as distinct from the explicit status that Christians commonly attributed to Jesus, the saying commends itself as authentic. It stands side by side with the saying from "Q" in asserting the dynamic incursion of the kingdom as a promise of its universal scope. Whether in exorcised demons or scarifying fire, the kingdom is portrayed as an intense intervention of God that cannot be contained. There is an affinity between the two images in that both involve purity (a coordinate that will concern us below). The removal of an unclean spirit establishes a person as pure; the story of the legion of demons illustrates that motif unforgettably (Matt. 8:28-34; Mark 5:1-20; Luke 8:26-39). Similarly, the purity of sacrifice within the covenant with Israel is marked by the presence of salt in what is offered by fire (Lev. 2:13).[19] Just as breaking the power of one demon dethrones them all, so the fire of the kingdom is uncontainable. Both images involve an intense manifestation of power that, once manifested, is not to be limited.

The Leaven of the Kingdom

The comparison of the kingdom of God to leaven is surprising. The image in itself is modest, especially as compared to the grandeur that is routinely attributed to the kingdom, and that modesty is underscored by the specific comparison of a *woman* "hiding" the yeast in the dough. A routine item is placed in a common food by a person so ordinary[20] and a gesture so unremarkable that the action is not noticeable. The consistency of the saying from "Q" in all its known versions (Matt. 13:33; Luke 13:20-21; *Thomas* 96)[21] and its stunning originality have led to

---

19. Most manuscripts of Mark 9:49 add a gloss explaining the image of salt in terms of sacrifice. The comment is in all probability not original (that is, not as a saying of Jesus), but it is accurate.

20. The specification "a woman" sets the action in a household rather than any sort of commercial bakery. It also raises potential issues of purity (which are discussed below).

21. See also 1 Cor. 5:6; Gal. 5:9.

the conclusion that it "transmits the voice of Jesus as clearly as any ancient record can."[22]

But the fact that Jesus made the comparison is no more significant than its radical view of transcendence. The local, sporadic incursion of the kingdom (already evident in Jesus' saying about his exorcisms) is generalized in the saying: the kingdom is hidden in gestures as common as the woman's. A cognitive challenge, to see the kingdom concealed in what is as ordinary as household dough, is implicit in the act of speaking the parable.[23] Seeing the kingdom in that way, manifest in one local — seemingly ordinary — incursion, also involves the anticipation that it will leaven everything that is ordinary.

Putting it in another way, we can say that the kingdom is so ordinary that it proves that everything is extraordinary. Just as the line between the usual and the unusual disappears in the light of the kingdom, so the local awareness of its hidden incursion points forward to its thorough leavening of the whole of experience. The transcendence of the kingdom is so thorough that Jesus sees it as permeating what can be seen and felt, and as by no means standing apart from experience, as if in an ideal realm.

Thomas 3 represents very clearly the tendency of the kingdom to transcend boundaries:

> If those who lead you say to you "See, the kingdom is in heaven," then the birds of heaven will precede you. If they say to you "It is in the sea," then the fish will precede you. But the kingdom is within you and outside you.

In the first part of the saying, Jesus warns his followers against the idea that the kingdom is only in a particular place. The method of argument here is *reductio ad absurdum*. When it is shown where an idea leads, the idea is discredited, as are the leaders who maintain it. Such syllogistic arguments can be effective, provided there are well-established conventions of abstract reasoning, but they are not elsewhere attributed to Jesus.

---

22. R. W. Funk, R. W. Hoover, and the Jesus Seminar, *The Five Gospels: The Search for the Authentic Words of Jesus* (New York: Macmillan, 1993) 195.

23. From the point of view of Aramaic usage, the saying is a parable (a *metala'*) because it involves a comparison.

In fact, the closest analogy in the Synoptic Gospels to the rhetoric of the argument in *Thomas* 3 is attributed not to Jesus but to his Sadducean opponents (Matt. 22:23-33; Mark 12:18-27; Luke 20:27-40). They set up a hypothetical question of a woman who marries a man, who then dies childless. Following the practice commanded in Deut. 25:5-6, his brother marries her to continue the deceased's name, but then he dies childless as well, as do his five remaining brothers. The point of this complicated scenario is to ridicule the idea of the resurrection of the dead by asking whose wife the woman will be in the resurrection. As in *Thomas* 3, the syllogism is designed to provoke mockery of the position that is attacked, and it depends on the prior acceptance of what it is reasonable to say and of how logic should be used. In short, both the Sadducees' argument and the argument of the "living Jesus" commend themselves to schoolmen and seem as far from the ethos of Jesus himself as the concern for what the leaders of churches might say. Those who would attribute the form of *Thomas* 3 to Jesus reveal only their own uncritical attachment to a source that is fashionable in certain circles simply because it is not canonical.

Although the form of *Thomas* 3 is artificial, it reflects Jesus' position to some extent. In statements in the Synoptics about the "Messiah" (so Matthew and Mark) or "the Son of man" (so Luke), Jesus warns against those who attempt to localize God's action in a limiting fashion (Matt. 24:23-24; Mark 13:21-22; Luke 17:23). The point at the close of saying 3 in *Thomas* is that the nature of the kingdom, "within you and outside you," resists limitation to a particular place. The coordinate of the kingdom's transcendence makes it impossible to localize; we are part of it more than we can perceive it, because its movement is within us and outside us.

The gist of the close of saying 3 is repeated and reformulated elsewhere in *Thomas* (see sayings 51 and 113); it is taken to be a basic part of the tradition. As a statement of the principle that makes the limitation of the kingdom impossible, it should be attributed to Jesus. Indeed, because Jesus held that the kingdom was transcendent in the sense of *Thomas* 3, he also insisted that the "Messiah" or "the Son of man" could not be localized. The kingdom of God constituted Jesus' fundamental theology, and it determined his perspective in regard to the theological questions of his time.

The transmission of an authentic saying of Jesus in *Thomas* 3 is also suggested by its relationship to a saying in Luke. There as well Jesus warns against those who claim that the kingdom is "here" or "there" because the kingdom of God is "in your midst" (Luke 17:21). Another translation of the saying would have the kingdom "within you," which has led to a serious misunderstanding. "Within you" in English is naturally taken as a purely interior possession, a mental realization of the kingdom. But the text of Luke has "you" in the plural and can only refer to a shared, communal reality.

The purpose of the assertion in Luke 17:21 is to contradict any assertion of an apocalyptic expectation of the kingdom to the effect that it would come only with signs (17:20). In the course of developing that purpose, the fuller version of Jesus' position, which asserts a kingdom both within and outside the hearers, has been truncated. Taken together, however, *Thomas* 3 and Luke 17:21 enable us to calibrate Jesus' fundamental insistence on the transcendence of the kingdom. His position has been expanded in *Thomas* to resist any local limitation of the kingdom and abbreviated in Luke to resist an apocalyptic limitation. Those developments were possible because it was clearly understood that Jesus saw local instances of the kingdom (in his exorcisms, in leaven) not as restrictions but as promises of what was to be everywhere.

Summary

The dynamic nature of the kingdom's transcendence in Jesus' understanding is demonstrated by his connection (in "Q") of its arrival to his own exorcisms. That arrival is far from comprehensive; it is as local and sporadic as the exit of unclean spirits, but the natural tendency of its arrival is that the kingdom will extend everywhere. The link between the kingdom and Jesus' activity more generally (that is, not only exorcism) is maintained in a probably authentic saying (82) from *Thomas*.

The transcendence of the kingdom, however, is such that its incursion may not be limited to Jesus' activity. Viewed correctly, it is as present as the leaven in bread, and its influence is as naturally extensive as yeast. As *Thomas* rightly represents Jesus' position, the kingdom is within us and outside us, so that Jesus' activity is to become a matter of general experience. It is not only that the kingdom is one day to be immanent; it is rather that the kingdom is already immanent and is one day to be comprehensive.

The Coordinate of Judgment

The ethical aspect of eschatology is as strong as the link within the literature of early Judaism between what God requires of his people and how he finally judges them. The distinctiveness of an eschatological speaker would lie in how he conceived the relationship between the coming judgment and the present imperative. Jesus saw the connection as so intimate that he viewed responsiveness to God as permitting one to "enter" his kingdom. Because the kingdom was usually conceived of eschatologically, Jesus' language of entering the kingdom was striking. He promised those who listened to him: Attend to the righteousness in which God rejoices and you come into the kingdom that you pray every day will come. The movement that climaxes in the encounter with God is not only God's responsibility, but ours.

Invitations to a Feast

The comparison of the kingdom of God to invitations to a feast receives development in a full narrative parable (Matt. 22:1-10; Luke 14:16-24; *Thomas* 64). Jesus tells a story of people's misguided attention to matters that are ordinarily seen as important. Consumed by the business of the day (in Matthew, even to the point of violence), they spurn the offer of a banquet that will not come around again. We have seen in chapter 3 that the motifs of the parable are also developed in Rabbinic literature. A similar parable is attributed to Yoḥanan ben Zakkai (a younger contemporary of Jesus) in which a king invited his servants to a feast, without announcing the hour of the meal.[24] Wise servants attired themselves properly and waited at the door of the king's house. Foolish servants expected definite signs of the meal's preparation and went about their work until they should see such signs. When the king appeared without further ado, the wise enjoyed a fine meal, and the foolish servants in their work-soiled clothing were allowed to enter, but were made to stand and watch while the others ate.

The essential emphasis of both Jesus' parable and Yoḥanan's par-

---

24. See Babylonian Talmud *Shabbat* 153 and the discussion in Bruce Chilton and J. I. H. McDonald, *Jesus and the Ethics of the Kingdom* (London: SPCK [in the series Biblical Foundations in Theology]/Grand Rapids: Eerdmans, 1987) 31-35.

able is on the overriding nature of the king's command: ordinary duties are superseded by the royal invitation. Indeed, once the king invites, attention to what is usually thought of as commendable activity is punished; nothing is to distract one from the feast, which has become one's goal. In its implicit conception of the kingdom, Jesus' parable (from "Q," once again in quite different versions in Matthew and Luke) presents no substantial difference from the parable attributed to Yohanan. In each, routine dutifulness is presented as an inhibition to entry into the kingdom. Moreover, the kingdom is viewed, from the point of view of judgment, as that into which one might or might not *enter*.

Entry into the kingdom is possible because it is already available as a transcendence that may even now be perceived (the second coordinate). Because the kingdom is currently within one's field of vision, devotion to mere duty — to anything that excludes the kingdom — can only slight the king. Once available, the kingdom can only be either entered or rejected.

The fundamental similarity between Jesus' parable and Yohanan's permits us to see by comparison those elements that are especially heightened in Jesus'. First, he names a wider range of activities that cause those invited to miss the appointed time of the invitation. Yohanan speaks only of people getting soiled working in the king's field; Jesus pictures people with farms and businesses (and extravagant weddings, in Luke and *Thomas*) of their own. The activities specified presuppose disposable wealth: a warning against riches is inherent in the parable (see also Matt. 19:23-34; Mark 10:23-25; Luke 18:24-25, discussed immediately below, and Jesus' saying concerning God and the Aramaic term "mammon," Matt. 6:24; Luke 16:13).[25] But although wealth is criticized in the parable, Jesus calls attention primarily to the consequence of wealth, the distractions it causes.[26]

In all three versions of Jesus' parable (each of which is distinctive), an unusual resistance to the king's invitation is also at issue. As Joachim Jeremias notes, sending servants out to escort guests to a feast was a

25. Discussed in B. Chilton, *A Galilean Rabbi and His Bible: Jesus' Use of the Interpreted Scripture of His Time* (Wilmington: Glazier, 1984), also published with the subtitle *Jesus' Own Interpretation of Isaiah* (London: SPCK, 1984) 117-123.

26. A similar concern is voiced in his parable of the sower in Matt. 13:1-9; Mark 4:1-9; Luke 8:4-8; *Thomas* 9.

special act of courtesy; the assumption of the parable is that those invited have long known of the feast.[27] Their obstinacy in refusing to attend a banquet they have long known of is another characteristic emphasis in Jesus' parable, along with his warning against the kind of distraction that wealth brings. Of course, their obstinacy and distraction are related. Activities that cause the invitation to be spurned (not merely declined) are by definition willful rejections of the feast, disastrous, self-imposed inhibitions from entering a household greater than one's own can ever be.

Against those inhibitions, Jesus' host offers a new invitation, one to those whose low status virtually assures their willingness to come. That willingness is all that commends them. They have not been more enthusiastic, more obedient, or more patient than those originally invited: their response is their only virtue. Where attentiveness is what Yohanan's parable insists on (at the cost of duty), Jesus' parable insists that rough alacrity will triumph over the business of the day.

That which is available, the feast whose invitations have already been issued, can either be accepted or rejected. The fact, in Jesus' understanding, that the transcendent kingdom is already immanent, that the king's servants have been sent to collect guests for the feast, means that judgment is already being worked out in terms of who agrees to be gathered in and who resists on the excuse of wealthy business.

The Eye of the Needle

Entry into the kingdom is also the dominant image in Jesus' famous statement about the rich, which derives from the Petrine source (Matt. 19:23-24; Mark 10:23-25; Luke 18:24). The parable just considered helps to illuminate why Jesus chose to target the rich as he did, and the possibilities of playing on words in Aramaic explains the rest:

27. See Joachim Jeremias, *The Parables of Jesus*, tr. S. H. Hooke (London: SCM, 1972) 176. Jeremias also (pp. 178-179) follows Gustav Dalman in the suggestion that Jesus might be alluding here to the story of the tax collector Bar Ma'yan, who was praised for inviting the poor to attend a feast when the councillors of the city, whom he had invited, failed to show up. An improved citation and discussion is available in Fritz Herrenbrück, *Jesus und die Zöllner* (Wissenschaftliche Untersuchungen zum Neuen Testament 41; Tübingen: Mohr, 1990) 213-215.

> Easier for a camel to wriggle through
> the eye of a needle *(ḥarara)*[28]
> than for a rich man to enter the kingdom *(malkhutha)* of God.

The play suggests itself because the picture of a big animal pushed through a needle's eye is a rabbinic figure of speech.[29] It is a type of expression that is used, for example, to refer to arguments that are so clumsy that they are ridiculous. *Ḥarar* means "litigation" in several of the Palestinian Aramaic texts edited by Joseph A. Fitzmyer and Daniel J. Harrington.[30] That secondary meaning makes the play on words in Jesus' saying possible: the eye of the needle for the camel is related to a ruinous lawsuit for a wealthy person.

A camel that passes through the eye of a needle is no longer a camel, and a rich man who enters the kingdom is no longer wealthy. By the time he has heeded the availability of the kingdom, he has put aside business to concern himself with the single royal invitation.[31]

Priceless Objects

Both Matthew (13:44, 45-46) and *Thomas* (sayings 109 and 76) present a pair of parables of Jesus that underscore the relationship between the kingdom and wealth. In doing so, they portray the kingdom as an object to be cherished (a treasure, a pearl) instead of as a realm to be entered. The two parables lay a basis for speaking of the kingdom in a new way as that which may be apprehended, grasped by those who

---

28. A form of the term is suggested in George M. Lamsa, *Gospel Light: Comments on the Teachings of Jesus from Aramaic and Unchanged Eastern Customs* (Philadelphia: Holman, 1939) 115-116. Lamsa uses later Syriac renderings of the Gospels as if they were contemporaneous with Jesus, and his work is not widely cited. But if one allows for the historical development of the language, some of his insights can be sustained. In the present case, I have reverted to the earlier Aramaic spelling.

29. See Babylonian Talmud *Berakhoth* 55b; *Baba Meṣi'a* 38b; *'Erubin* 53a.

30. See *A Manual of Palestinian Aramaic Texts* (Biblica et Orientalia 34; Rome: Biblical Institute Press, 1978).

31. Vincent Taylor "deprecated" attempts to rationalize the saying, for example by imagining that a door in a wall in Jerusalem might have been called "the eye of the needle" and that a camel might just have squeezed through it. The (for Taylor) tough language is appropriate, and such interpretations miss the point of the parable. See *The Gospel according to St. Mark* (London: Macmillan, 1966) 431.

are willing to take the opportunity of converting their wealth into a greater value.

The kingdom is compared to a treasure hidden in a field; a man finds it, conceals it, and then happily spends everything to buy the field and gain the treasure (Matt. 13:44). The version in *Thomas* 109 is elaborated by means of narrative: A man has a hidden treasure in his field and dies without knowing it or explaining to the heir. Unaware of the value of the property, the son sells the field, to the advantage of the lucky buyer. The saying is a good example of a didactic warning within the Church long after Jesus of what happens when one does not pay attention to the kingdom.[32] It is similar in its warning to the parable of the sower (Matt. 13:3-9; Mark 4:3-9; Luke 8:5-8; *Thomas* 9), which is widely acknowledged to have been attributed to Jesus in its present form only late in the tradition. Both the parable of the sower and *Thomas*'s version of the parable of the treasure assume that Jesus' followers already possess the treasure and that they need to accept the discipline of the Church in order to retain it. The point of the original parable is that the commercial opportunity of finding *unexpected* treasure makes one wily: one purchases the field without a thought for the rights of the owner.

Similarly — and less dishonestly — finding the finest pearl will cause a merchant to sell up in order to buy it (Matt. 13:45-46; *Thomas* 76). In this case, *Thomas* may present the more original version in not making the merchant a dealer in pearls. That makes the joy of finding the pearl and the risk involved in acquiring it all the more striking. But in both parables and in both versions (Matthew's and *Thomas*'s), the kingdom presents itself as a surprising opportunity, of which one naturally and aggressively takes advantage.

Both Matthew and *Thomas* derive from Syrian traditions; Matthew was composed in Damascus and *Thomas* (almost a century later) in Edessa. Their sharing of a distinct (probably oral) source of Jesus' teaching explains why they preserve the parables of the hidden treasure and the pearl while the other Gospels do not. Matthew and *Thomas* both took the portrayal of the kingdom as an object in quite new directions that were not characteristic of Jesus' thought. (Those developments will concern us in chapter 6.) But their use of their Syrian source enables us to see how Jesus could change his grounding metaphor from entry

---

32. The motif is also developed in a parable attributed to a rabbi of the second century, Simeon ben Yoḥai, in Midrash Rabbah, Song of Songs 4.12.1.

to possession in order to explain the fresh opportunity of the kingdom. The idea of acquiring the transcendent kingdom was not taken up generally in the traditions of the Gospels, but it was just the sort of paradox in which Jesus took pleasure. He presses it to its extremes in his saying about taking the kingdom of God as a child (Mark 10:15; Luke 18:17), which will concern us in our discussion of the fourth coordinate of the kingdom, and in his saying about people actually laying hold of the kingdom of God (Luke 16:16; Matt. 11:12), which will concern us in our discussion of the fifth coordinate of the kingdom.

Summary

Jesus saw the kingdom of God as already present in the experience of those who listened to him. The eschatological coordinate of his usage insisted that what was final was now certain, just as the transcendent coordinate conceived of the kingdom as immanent, although occasional. Both of those aspects of usage implied that the kingdom's judgment was under way. In the sayings classed under the coordinate of judgment, entry into the kingdom and acquisition of the kingdom are both cast as current opportunities.

Different though the two grounding metaphors may appear to be, both envisage contact between a person and the kingdom at the moment of that person's committed response. Along the line of the grounding metaphor of entry, one accepts an invitation, dropping all manner of usual duties; one wriggles through the needle's eye. In both instances, one enters the kingdom, leaving behind both wealth and less daring companions. Along the line of the grounding metaphor of acquisition, one angles for treasure on the pretext of buying a field; one sells off merchandise for the loveliest pearl. Either way, one's wealth is spent, and the joy of possession cannot be shared by those who did not appreciate what was available.

The coordinate of judgment is what introduces into Jesus' sayings a tendency that (ironically) seems lacking in dignity and sometimes even less than moral. Much as Yoḥanan ben Zakkai's king praised servants who did nothing but wait, Jesus' host wanted fellowship without regard to the status of his guests. The shedding of wealth is enjoined in the parable of the camel, and yet Jesus commends both a wily speculator who seizes treasure and a merchant who gambles everything on a single pearl.[33] In every case, one is either squeezing into the kingdom or grasping at it, and breaking ordinary rules in order to do so. Subversion of conventional morality is inevitable if what is final and transcendent has become available within one's experience. That availability then becomes an occasion greater than any other, an opportunity in comparison with which any wealth or any status is only of instrumental worth. Everything else is there to be disposed of in the attempt to squeeze into the narrow gate (Matt. 7:13-14; Luke 13:23-24, from "Q") or to capitalize on the talents one has been given (Matt. 25:14-30; Luke 19:11-27, also from "Q").

The Coordinate of Purity

Purity is at issue whenever there is a definition of what persons, what actions, or what objects are compatible with the divine. Jesus engaged in that task of definition, both explicitly and implicitly. Examples include his cleansing of a leper (Matt. 8:2-4; Mark 1:40-44; Luke 5:12-14) and his declaration of what defiles a person (Matt. 15:11; Mark 7:15).[34] But the practice that most distinguished Jesus from other teachers was his manner of eating socially.

The meal of the group with Jesus constituted a circle of purity, whose acceptability to the divine was asserted by associating that social meal with the kingdom of God. Jesus accepted that others called him a glutton and a drunkard, a friend of those whom many Pharisees despised, because he ate and drank as a characteristic activity (Matt. 11:19; Luke 7:34). He also commissioned some of his disciples to engage in such a program (Matt. 10:11-14; Mark 6:10; Luke 9:4). In the next chapter, the practice of social eating as an activity commissioned by Jesus will be discussed; the present concern is with how purity is portrayed as a coordinate of the kingdom.

---

33. From the perspective of these sayings it is not surprising that Jesus would also commend a dishonest steward. Cf. Luke 16:1-9 and my discussion in *A Galilean Rabbi and His Bible*, 116-123.

34. For other examples, and discussion, see Chilton, *The Temple of Jesus: His Sacrificial Program within a Cultural History of Sacrifice* (University Park: Pennsylvania State University, 1992), chapter 7: "The Sacrificial Program of Jesus," 113-136.

Gathering from East and West in the Kingdom of God

A prominent image employed by Jesus, attested in varying forms in the source called "Q" (Matt. 8:11-12; Luke 13:28-29), pictures people being gathered from east and west in order to feast with Abraham, Isaac, and Jacob in the kingdom of God. It has been argued that the reference to east and west implies that people beyond the boundaries of Israel are to be included in the eschatological banquet. So understood, the image is a promise of "the Gentiles' share in the salvation of the Messianic age."[35] That reading identifies how the saying could have been understood among those in the Church who later faced the issue of how Jews and non-Jews are to be related, but Jesus' saying was distinct from that concern of the Church in the Greco-Roman world.

Jesus' movement centered in Galilee and was characterized by fellowship at meals involving various people with different practices of purity. His circle needed to cope with the issue of defilement as one member of Israel (with a certain set of practices) met with another member of Israel (with another set of practices). To deal with that question, a single aphorism of Jesus was precisely designed:

> Nothing that is outside a person entering one defiles one,
> except that things coming from a person, these defile one.[36]

As Jesus saw the matter, once one is identified with Israel, it is not what is without that defiles, but those things that come from oneself.

The second line of the aphorism makes it clear that originally its meaning was not limited to food, since many things proceed from a person that have nothing to do with his alimentary canal. The limitation to food is accomplished by the packaging of the saying within the Hellenistic concerns of the Gospels, where the controlling issue is whether or not hands are to be washed (see Matt. 15:1-2; Mark 7:1-5). Jesus' point was rather that contagion from impurity was a matter of what one did, not one's contacts. Separation from that which is outside

---

35. So Joachim Jeremias, *Jesus' Promise to the Nations*, tr. S. H. Hooke (Studies in Biblical Theology 24; London: SCM, 1958) 62.

36. The rendering is of the Aramaic proverb that I have identified behind the Greek text of Mark 7:14-15. See "A Generative Exegesis of Mark 7:1-23," *Journal for the Study of Higher Criticism* (forthcoming).

one does not therefore assure purity, and non-Jews in the mixed environment of Galilee pose no particular danger to Israel.

The circle of Jesus frames its rhetoric for its specific social circumstance in Galilee: Israel in the midst of the nations.[37] Defilement here is a matter of failing to recognize the others of Israel, refusing to share with the pure Israel that those others represent. Jesus' concern with Israel in the midst of non-Jews led to his conviction that their non-Jewish environment did not compromise the identity of Israel.

That conviction was transmuted at a later stage into the equally firm insistence — by Paul and those like him — that in Christian gatherings the distinction between Jew and Greek no longer matters (Gal. 3:28). That stance of Hellenistic Christianity could only be developed in the Greco-Roman world once non-Jewish constituents of the movement were so significant that they could challenge the assumption that ordinary Judaic practices of purity were to be honored. Jesus' position was worked out at too early a stage to be a simple matter of universalism. He at no point challenged the identity of Israel as the people of God, and he assumed that purity and sacrifice in the Temple would be matters of concern for those who listened to him.

His focus on Israel in the midst of nations explains the force of Jesus' promise that peoples will come from east and west in order to feast with the patriarchs. The imagery was inspired by the book of Zechariah, which also pictures God as gathering his people from east and west (Zech. 8:7). The purpose of the gathering is to bring them to Jerusalem, to know their God in that place (Zech. 8:8) and to join in feasting (v. 19). Zechariah sees the exemplary value of the feast as so strong that even non-Jews will seek to join themselves to the presence of God (vv. 20-23).

Jesus shared the Zecharian vision that Israel's gathering would draw in those beyond Israel. His development of motifs and language from the book of Zechariah, by means of his statements and his activities, will draw our attention in chapter 5. But he did not articulate that vision by claiming — in the Pauline manner — that the distinction between Israel and the nations no longer existed. His entire approach was to focus on the assembly of Israel as the hope of all.

37. See Seán Freyne, "The Geography, Politics, and Economics of Galilee and the Quest for the Historical Jesus," *Studying the Historical Jesus: Evaluations of the State of Current Research*, ed. Chilton and C. A. Evans (New Testament Tools and Studies 19; Leiden: Brill, 1994) 75-121.

Taking the Kingdom of God as a Child

Jesus' famous saying about imitating a child (Mark 10:15; Luke 18:17) and entering the kingdom is a promise cast as a threat. Behaving like a child is implicitly commended, but the structure of the conditional statement is overtly pointed against a failure to act like a child:

> Whoever does not take the kingdom of God as a child
> will never enter it.

The orientation is toward what one does or does not do: is it as a child *does?* The issue is not what one is. That orientation is sometimes obscured because the later formulation in Matthew (18:3) demands that the community (addressed in the plural) "turn" and "become" as children. The imagery in Matthew serves the context of conversion and baptism within the Church[38] more than it reflects the attempt of Jesus (better represented in Mark and Luke) to identify how the kingdom might be entered.

Confusion has also been produced by the translation of the Greek term *dechomai,* which I have rendered as "take." English translations since the King James Version have typically used "receive" here.[39] Tonally (especially in English), there is an important difference between simply taking what one wants and receiving what one has been offered. *Dechomai* will bear either meaning, depending on the context that is involved.

Relating the saying to another well-known statement of Jesus makes it quite clear what context Jesus had in mind. He complains in a saying from "Q," which has already been mentioned (p. 80 above), that people call John crazy for abstaining from food and drink and call Jesus a glutton and a drunkard because he eats and drinks with people. People of that kind, he says, are like children in a marketplace squabbling over whether they should play happy games or sad games (Matt. 11:16-19; Luke 7:31-35). Jesus' perspective on children was unromantic; he knows they argue, just as he knows they take what they want.

39. The rendering of the King James Version is apposite: "Except ye be converted and become as little children. . . ."

40. *The Five Gospels* chooses "accept," a distinction from the conventional rendering without any difference in tonality.

The apparently more polite rendering, "receive the kingdom of God," runs the risk here of dissolving the statement into the banality that we should be like well-behaved children. The view has even been championed that "receiving the kingdom of God as a child" means embracing the kingdom as one would a child, rather than taking it as a child takes.[40] Jesus' usage of the metaphor involved comparison with unruly activity, not polite passivity. The Aramaic term he employed was probably *teqep*,[41] a term that features in another of his sayings (see the discussion below of Matt. 11:12-13; Luke 16:16, pp. 94-96) and that vividly conveys the image of taking, as a child seizes what he wants.

By seizing the kingdom as a child takes something to play with, one can enter the kingdom. The ethic of grabbing the kingdom is also reflected in sayings classed under the coordinate of judgment, and the two grounding metaphors that we saw in those sayings(see p. 79 above), entering the kingdom and laying hands on it, are juxtaposed here. Indeed, the parable of the grabby child manifests considerable aphoristic skill in relating those two models in a single statement and in showing how they are related to one another. Making the kingdom one's sole object of interest, the way a child fixes on a toy or on a forbidden object, makes one pure enough to enter the kingdom.

Once the saying was passed on in the Petrine cycle of tradition, it became natural for the image of a child to to be associated with Christian initiation and even Christian leadership. Mark (10:13-14, 16) and Luke (18:15-16) place Jesus' aphorism in a story about children being presented to him, while Matthew — as we have seen — employs the language of repentance ("unless you turn and become as children"), in order to speak of the necessary humility of Jesus' baptized followers (18:1-5).[42]

Contextually, *Thomas* (saying 22) combines both of these later issues (leadership and initiation) in its presentation of the saying. Mary is presented as asking about the disciples in the previous saying, and Jesus replies with an image of children in saying 21. They remove their

---

40. For a discussion of such possibilities and further treatment of the symbolism involved and variations among the texts, see *Jesus and the Ethics of the Kingdom*, 83-89.

41. For the sense of the term, see *God in Strength*, 226-230.

42. The greater interest of Matthew's Gospel in the order of the community is well known; see Günther Bornkamm, "End-Expectation and Church in Matthew," in G. Bornkamm, G. Barth, and H. J. Held, *Tradition and Interpretation in Matthew*, tr. P. Scott (New Testament Library; London: SCM, 1963) 15-51.

clothes as an act of witness when they return a field they have inhabited to its actual owners. The import of the material is that the disciples are compared to children because they lack shame in regard to sexuality, but at the same time they are understanding and know how to protect themselves from the world by abstinence. Indeed, the image of children is then dropped, to be replaced with a version of the parable of the wise householder who knows how to defend his property (see Matt. 24:43; Luke 12:39) and an allusion to the parable of the alert harvester (see Mark 4:26-29). Then comes a saying about suckling children entering the kingdom in saying 22 itself, and finally Jesus says that one will enter the kingdom upon being united with one's heavenly image, that is, upon baptism. The combination and development of material is quite obviously both sophisticated and derivative.

Baptism is not the context in Jesus' original saying. Rather, children are the image of the confusing, grabby, unruly way in which the kingdom is to be greeted. The picture of children in the marketplace, hard at disorderly play, also appears in the book of Zechariah (8:5): their shrieks are signs of God's return to Jerusalem.[43] Jesus evokes that sign in his saying about squabbling children (Matt. 11:16-17; Luke 7:32),[44] just as his language about people coming from east and west to feast in the kingdom (Matt. 8:11; Luke 13:29) is evocative of the Zecharian language of how God is to gather his people (Zech. 8:7). In Jesus' conception the purity required by the kingdom is a purity of response, of being like children at rough play in grasping at the kingdom.

New Wine in the Kingdom

Jesus' practice of an inclusive definition of purity at meals involved a radical acceptance of the produce of all Israel as pure and an equally radical acceptance of all those who might join his fellowship, whether encountered locally or on journeys, as children of Abraham.[45] The emblematic statement that provides the rationale of Jesus' program is

43. In the Hebrew text, boys and girls are said to be *meśaḥqim*, which refers to noisy laughter and sport.

44. The connection of the children in the marketplace with the children in Zechariah has often been made.

45. That appears to be the policy reflected, albeit indirectly, in Matt. 3:9/Luke 3:8; Luke 13:16; 16:19-31; 19:9.

the image of all Israel joining Abraham, Isaac, and Jacob in festal eating in the kingdom of God (Matt. 8:11, 12/Luke 13:28, 29). The paradigmatic link between the kingdom and fellowship at meals is widely accepted as an established feature of what Jesus taught,[46] and with ample warrant (cf. Matt. 22:1-14/Luke 14:15-24; Matt. 20:21/Mark 10:37).

Meals in Jesus' fellowship became practical parables whose meaning was as evocative as his verbal parables (which have consumed much more scholarly attention). To join in his meals consciously was, in effect, to anticipate the kingdom as it had been delineated by Jesus' teaching. Each meal was a proleptic celebration of God's kingdom; the promise of the next was also an assurance of the kingdom. There is, then, a certain inevitability in the saying "I will not again drink of the fruit of the vine, until I drink it new in the kingdom of God" (cf. Matt. 26:29/Mark 14:25 and Luke 22:16, 18). Quite outside the context of what came to be known as "the last supper," the practice of fellowship at meals in Jesus' movement in its formative period forged a link with the kingdom such that the promise of God's final disclosure on behalf of his people was as ardently and carelessly anticipated as the next dinner.

The saying asserts, in effect, the resolve only to drink of the fruit of the vine in conscious anticipation of the kingdom, within the fellowship of restored purity that Jesus' meals established. Its meaning may be compared to the request for daily bread in the Lord's Prayer, which follows the petition regarding the kingdom (Matt. 6:11/Luke 11:3). In both cases God's ultimate revelation is associated with the anticipation of an act of humble eating. The request for bread in the Lord's Prayer is linked to the kingdom in the private context of petitions for forgiveness and constancy, while the new wine of the kingdom is a more vigorous assurance in the communal context of a meal. Within Jesus' movement, the bread that sustains us and the wine that rejoices us are taken as a foretaste and warrant of the kingdom that transforms us.

The interpretation of the promise of the kingdom's new wine has been governed by the assumption that the construction is designed to convey a rigidly temporal meaning. It is taken to mean: I will fast until the kingdom comes, and then I will drink. That is a possible sense, and one can see, for example, in Luke 2:26 that such a promise might be

---

46. Cf. Otfried Hofius, *Jesu Tischgemeinschaft mit den Sündern* (Calwer: Stuttgart, 1967).

current: Simeon is not to die until he has seen the Messiah, but he is to die after he does see the Messiah (whom the narrative assumes is Jesus). But the statement actually says that he is not to die *before* that event, and it is a unique occurrence in the New Testament.[47]

Such a reading of Jesus' statement, as if it were like Simeon's, forces us to presuppose that Jesus is self-consciously eating a last supper prior to his death and refusing to drink until the feast of the kingdom. Even if one grants both that Jesus' saying was only uttered at the last supper and at no earlier meal and that he proceeded on the basis of a personal insight that he was about to die, the narrative reading remains implausible. Who would claim that Jesus knew precisely how many meals he would celebrate in his fellowship prior to his execution? Although that degree of foresight is not generally ascribed to Jesus today, it is necessary for the narrative hypothesis. Jesus must say these words at his *last* supper, and he must *know* it is his last; any additional act of eating with others would push that supper out of last position.

The problems of the narrative reading do not end there. In addition to being implausible, it is simply contradicted by the Synoptic narrative itself. According to Matt. 27:34 and Mark 15:23, Jesus was given wine immediately prior to the crucifixion[48] in accordance with a humane custom in Jerusalem.[49] Even on the assumption that a sip of wine would not break the promise, the contradiction is fatal to the usual reading and its many suppositions: after all, if Jesus knew he was to be executed and how many meals he would have before he died, he ought to have been familiar with the practice of giving prisoners drugged wine prior to capital punishment. The offer of vinegar to him on the cross (Matt. 27:48; Mark 15:36; Luke 23:36) only compounds the difficulty.

Instead of reading it as a narrative of Jesus' last acts in advance, the saying might be taken temporally, but in an eschatological sense, to

47. See Joseph A. Fitzmyer, *The Gospel According to Luke (I–IX)* (Anchor Bible; Garden City: Doubleday, 1981) 422, 427.

48. Both Gospels add that he did not accept drinking it fully, in order not to present him as breaking his apparent resolution. Luke avoids the difficulty by omitting the reference.

49. See Babylonian Talmud *Sanhedrin* 43a; Joachim Jeremias, *Jerusalem in the Time of Jesus,* tr. F. H. and C. H. Cave (London: SCM, 1969) 95. The Talmudic passage refers to providing wine with frankincense to one who is led out to execution (cf. Prov. 31:6). Noble women in Jerusalem are held customarily to donate the drink.

mean that Jesus resolved never to drink wine *at all.* The plausibility of such a temporal reading is even less defensible than the narrative proposal. The wine given to Jesus at the crucifixion remains a contradiction, and in addition the festal imagery of eating and drinking — a topos of divine disclosure in early Judaism that is as vivid as the prophecy of Isaiah (25:6-8) and as primordial as the sacrificial meal of Melchizedek (Gen. 14:18-20) — would be denied. Because the usage of the festal imagery of the kingdom was central to Jesus' message, the eschatological reading of his promise not to drink wine may safely be rejected.

What has made the saying difficult to understand in the history of scholarship is that its Semitic syntax has not been appreciated. That syntax need not be rigidly connected to a notion of time, as we have already seen in the exegesis of the promise of the kingdom as warranted by those who will never taste death (pp. 62-65 above).[50] Just as God performing what he swore to Jacob in Gen. 28:15 cannot involve God abandoning Jacob in any sense, so the point of Jesus' saying is the image of consuming new wine in the kingdom (cf. Matt. 9:16, 17; Mark 2:21, 22; Luke 5:36-39) rather than not drinking any wine in the present. It is designed principally to assure the hearer that the wine of the kingdom is soon to be enjoyed.

The saying belongs to a definite syntactical type, which derives from the Semitic construction already mentioned, utilizing "not" *(lo')* and "until" *('ad).* Jesus' warrants of this type, which employ the emphatic negative *ou mē* (for *lo'*) and *heōs* with or without *an* (for *'ad*), generally envisage that the condition initially posited will endure. For example, he warns that a person going to prison will not get out until the last penny has been paid (Matt. 5:25, 26; Luke 12:58, 59). The point, of course, is not that payment will secure release; rather, he warns that Roman justice will impoverish those who appeal to it, with no easy escape for those who are entangled in it. By analogy, Jesus' emphasis in the saying about drinking wine new in the kingdom is on that eschatological feast that is to include his followers, and a corollary sense of the saying is that Jesus will drink wine only in the fellowship of those meals that celebrate the kingdom.

---

50. For full discussion see *A Feast of Meanings,* Appendix 2: "The Construction οὐ μή . . . ἕως [ἄv] in Asseverations of Jesus," 169-176; Klaus Beyer, *Semitische Syntax im Neuen Testament* (Studien zur Umwelt des Neuen Testaments 1; Göttingen: Vandenhoeck und Ruprecht, 1962) 132, 133 (n. 1). Cf. *God in Strength,* pp. 268-272, where the analysis is applied to Mark 9:1, as in "The Transfiguration: Dominical Assurance and Apostolic Vision," *New Testament Studies* 27 (1980) 115-124.

In the Synoptics the ordering of the promise inside the artificial framework of the Passion means that Jesus' assertion is taken as a vow. Matthew (27:34) and Mark (15:23) have him all but refuse a drink given him prior to crucifixion, but then accept another on the cross (Matt. 27:48; Mark 15:36). Although the presentation is flawed, as we have seen, the construal of his promise of the new wine as a vow is understandable. A similar form of what must be taken as a vow is evidenced in Acts 23:12, 21.[51]

Matthew and Mark therefore manifest a tendency of interpretation, without actually making Jesus' saying into a simple vow that he actually kept. Luke is another matter. The saying concerning eating the Passover in Luke 22:16 reads a different form of words for "until": *heōs hotou* appears instead of *heōs an*. That tiny change makes the form much more like the explicit vow in the book of Acts. In Luke 22:18, *heōs hou* in the statement concerning drinking wine makes the identification with the form of the vow in Acts complete. Verbally, the Lukan Jesus is refusing to eat or drink until the kingdom should come. And the distinction of Luke from Matthew and Mark is not only a matter of linguistic presentation. Luke also omits reference to the giving of what Mark calls myrrhed wine (15:23) and what Matthew calls wine with gall (27:34), so that the issue of Jesus breaking his vow does not arise. Similarly, Luke (23:36) has a soldier (rather than a bystander) only offer Jesus vinegar, while in Matthew (27:48) and Mark (15:36) the drink is actually given.

In aggregate, the Synoptics present the promise of new wine as a hero's vow of abstinence, and that results in either inconsistencies (so Matthew and Mark) or considerable recasting of the traditional materials (so Luke).[52] The vow of heroic abstinence, which is barely kept in Luke and is apparently broken in Matthew and Mark, is a consequence of the Synoptic ordering, not of Jesus' anticipation of the kingdom in the purity of his meals. For him, *every* act of fellowship in expectation of the divine rule was an assurance that the kingdom that he prayed for would come. Matt. 26:29 and Mark 14:25 represent a statement that

51. In both cases in Acts, however, *heōs hou* is used instead of *heōs . . . hotan* (compare Mark 14:25; Matt. 26:29). The distinction marks the original (and major) difference of meaning between an assurance and a vow.

52. The liturgical interest of Luke, in pairing the vow concerning wine in 22:18 with the vow concerning the Passover in 22:16, manifests the way in which earlier Petrine material was developed in Antioch, probably under the influence of the apostle Barnabas.

Jesus might have made during any celebration of mealtime fellowship in celebration of God's kingdom. Ordering them into a "last supper" is an artificial development that imputes to the words an altogether different meaning.

Summary

Just as baptism has shaped the understanding of the saying that urges us to take the kingdom as a child takes things (Mark 10:15; Luke 18:17), so eucharist has shaped the understanding of the promise of new wine (Matt. 26:29; Mark 14:25; Luke 22:16, 18). In both cases, the meaning of Jesus, promising and anticipating that purity that God requires and enjoys (Matt. 8:11-12; Luke 13:28-29), remains recoverable. His point is not that children have a privileged status or that eucharistic practice should be associated with asceticism, although those meanings were developed in the early Church. Rather, Jesus insisted on recognition of the purity that derived from within Israel as a matter of the identity of the people of God (Mark 7:14-15). That was the basis on which — in Jesus' understanding as in Zechariah's (Zech. 8:7) — God was gathering his people. The feast with Abraham, Isaac, and Jacob was for Jesus the practice of the kingdom as well as the promise of the kingdom.

The Coordinate of Radiation

Because the kingdom tends toward transcendence and judgment, the notion that it is in some sense radiant is implicit. But the radiance of the kingdom is not merely implicit; our consideration of usages in the Psalms (pp. 40-42 above) showed a deliberate focus on the recognition of the kingdom, centered in Zion, by peoples outside of Israel. Zechariah 8, which we have just now seen to have inspired Jesus' understanding of purity, closes with a climactic prediction of non-Jews seeking God in Jerusalem with the aid of Jews (vv. 20-23).

Overt universalism, of course, was embraced in early Christianity. The language in which it was expressed might be Pauline, denying that any distinction existed between Jew and non-Jew (Gal. 3:28), or it might be Matthean, utilizing the more traditional language of reaching out to the nations (Matt. 28:19). But in either form early Christian universalism is striking for two reasons. First, it is vehemently claimed to represent the significance of Jesus after the resurrection. But second, it is not attributed to Jesus during the time of his ministry.

The Matthean commission to "make disciples of all nations" in 28:19 is the imperative of the risen Jesus. His earlier commands were to seek only "the lost sheep of the house of Israel" to the exclusion of others (10:6; 15:24). Matthew together with Mark passes on the story in which Jesus implicitly compares a non-Jewish woman and her daughter to dogs (Matt. 15:21-28; Mark 7:24-30). Similarly, the same Paul who insists that in Christ Jesus "there is neither Jew nor Greek" (Gal. 3:28) also acknowledges that the Jesus who was powerfully designated son of God by the resurrection was also descended from David "according to flesh" (Rom. 1:3-4).

In their differing ways, both the Matthean and the Pauline constructions of Christian universalism acknowledge that Jesus' own activity was more limited than the significance that they attribute to it. Local restriction and unlimited range are both implicitly involved in Jesus' position, whether represented by Matthew or by Paul. That paradox plays at the center of Jesus' own conception of the kingdom's radiance.

The Mustard Seed

Among the parables of Jesus, the comparison of the kingdom with the mustard seed precisely reflects the juxtaposition between the local and the unlimited. Its presentation in all three Synoptic Gospels (Matt. 13:31-32; Mark 4:30-32; Luke 13:18-19), as well as in *Thomas* (saying 20), is a consequence of its central place in two primitive cycles of tradition, the Petrine source and "Q." The Petrine source (reflected in Mark 4:30-32) envisages the tiny mustard seed making "big branches"; "Q" has the seed becoming "a tree" (Matt. 13:31-32; Luke 13:18-19). *Thomas* 20 represents a hybrid of the two versions and has Jesus refer to the seed as putting forth "a great plant."[53] In all the earliest represen-

---

53. Great size is used in *Thomas* as an image of what is cherished by God. Thus the wise fisherman chooses only one large fish from his net (saying #8), and the lost sheep is the largest (saying #107).

tations of the parable, the contrast between the small seed and the great result, which offers the birds shelter, is the evident emphasis.

In his classic discussion of the parable, Joachim Jeremias pairs the mustard seed with the parable of the leaven and concludes that the "meaning is that out of the most insignificant beginnings, invisible to human eye, God creates his mighty Kingdom, which embraces all the people of the world."[54] But the image of the birds is more adequately treated in Jeremias's book *Jesus' Promise to the Nations:*[55]

> The parable of the mustard seed, then, is another expression of the conception of the eschatological pilgrimage of the Gentiles when it speaks of the host of birds which nest in the shelter of the mustard bush.

In its specific reference to Gentiles, Jeremias's analysis is strained. He argues that the verb "shelter" is "an eschatological technical term" because it is used in *Joseph and Aseneth* 15:7. But that usage, in a work that in any case may be later than the New Testament, is an explicit reference to non-Jewish people sheltered by God in view of their repentance. It is "technical" only because *Joseph and Aseneth* treats the issue of conversion to Judaism at length. Although Jeremias was right to stress the importance of response to the kingdom among the concerns of the parable, his attempt to identify the birds with non-Jews was not successful.

In fact, there is no plain reference in the parable of the mustard seed to "the eschatological pilgrimage of the Gentiles" or to a kingdom that "embraces all the people of the world." The imagery is, rather, reminiscent of Ps. 104:10-17, where God's provision in creation provides birds and other animals with shelter. But where Psalm 104 is expressly cosmological, a hymn to the might of divine power and its celebration in the Temple,[56] Jesus' parable emphasizes the minute size of the seed that brings about a mighty result. For Jesus, the counterpart on earth of the infinite range of God's power is not the Temple or Jerusalem but the tiny seed of the parable, which can be any and each tiny seed.

---

54. *The Parables of Jesus,* 149. The reading is the same in the ninth German edition, *Die Gleichnisse Jesu* (Göttingen: Vandenhoeck und Ruprecht, 1977) 148.

55. P. 69.

56. The similarity to the usage of Ps. 103:19 (from the fourth, eschatological stage of the book of Psalms), discussed below in Appendix 2 (p. 162), is striking.

The local instance of the kingdom is the seed, and its acknowledgment grows wherever it is permitted to prosper. The radiance of the kingdom is a matter of growth upward and outward, and of the response of the birds that use what grows to nest in. The situation is similar in the imagery of a plant and nesting in Ezek. 17:22-24. There, too, God's planting offers birds the shadow of its branches, and their acceptance of the shelter is part of God's radiant victory. But that victory is clearly for the kingdom of Judah.[57] Universal recognition of God's power is not the equivalent of universal inclusion in the kingdom.

Just as there is no express universalism in the birds, so there is no express theology of Zion (as in the Psalms) in the mustard seed. Why should Jesus have resorted to indeterminacy? Why not say simply, as in Isaiah 2 and Zechariah 8, that God would gather all the peoples of the earth to Zion? Had he done so, Jeremias would be obviously right. The focus on the Temple and the inclusion of the Gentiles would then be explicit. In the course of Jesus' occupation of the Temple, which is analyzed in the next chapter, Mark has Jesus say (11:17):

> My house shall be called a house of prayer
> *for all the nations,*
> but you have made it a den of thieves.

The authenticity of this saying is manifest: it indicates an enduring interest in the Temple, not the withdrawal from it that became a hallmark of non-Judaic Christianity. In the midst of his insistence on proper worship in the Temple, Jesus would naturally have used the "den of thieves" metaphor from Jer. 7:11, as well as the "house of prayer" language of Isa. 56:7. But the specific assurance that "all the nations" are to be included in that house of prayer is not to be found in Matt. 21:13 or Luke 19:46.[58]

---

57. See Moshe Greenberg, *Ezekiel 1–20* (Anchor Bible 22; Garden City: Doubleday, 1983) 319-320. The image of a tree for Nebuchadnezzar's kingdom is seen in Dan. 4:10-12, 20-22. Evidently the metaphor could be applied in a variety of ways and was not restricted to Judah. Among the usages cited here, the reference of the image to God is most explicit in Psalm 104 and in Jesus' parable of the mustard seed.

58. In fact, the language is derived from Isa. 56:7 itself; but the promise there is for foreigners who convert (see 56:6). For a discussion of the question, see *The Temple of Jesus,* 116, 119 and Craig Evans, *Jesus and His Contemporaries* (Leiden: Brill, 1995) 362-365.

Jesus did not or would not spell out what could easily have been specified, so Jeremias's argument is finally untenable. Jesus' unique emphasis in the parable is on the nature of the kingdom's radiance, on how it shines out from the seed in the earth and is reflected in the nesting of hungry birds. The point(s) from which it shines and the destination of its beams are not addressed in the parable.

The Available Kingdom

No saying of Jesus has been the subject of more disagreement than his statement regarding the kingdom of God since the time of John the Baptist. Even Matthew (11:12) and Luke (16:16) present the wording in quite different forms, probably because "Q" already circulated in distinct versions by the time the two Gospels were composed:

Matthew:
    a) From the days of John the Baptist until now
    b) the kingdom of the heavens breaks in violently
    c) and violent men take it hostage.

Luke:
    a) The law and the prophets were until John, from then
    b) the kingdom of God is preached
    c) and everyone breaks violently into it.

Both Matthew and Luke, as we shall see, help us to appreciate what the initial saying must have been, but the first question to be answered is why they use such different words to describe both the kingdom and people's reaction to it. By working systematically through the three parts of the saying, the meanings that Matthew and Luke attribute to it become plain.

The more stately assertion about John in Matthew (a) is present because the saying has been placed in a speech about John (Matt. 11:7-19). For that reason, the reference to the law and the prophets has been delayed until the next verse (v. 13), which simply says that all the prophets and the law prophesied until John. Because Jesus initially belonged to John's movement of purity by means of baptism, it is not surprising that he should have seen John as the point from which God's kingdom was especially available. The reference to the law and the prophets in association with John, as in Luke's version of (a), makes that point tellingly.

In the next part of the saying (b), however, Luke's diction ("is preached," *euangelizetai*) looks pale in comparison to Matthew's ("breaks in violently," *biazetai*). What could have produced such different understandings of the meaning of the statement? An Aramaic term that has already concerned us (*teqep*, p. 84) provides the answer. *Tēqēp*, whose basic meaning is "take" or "grasp," may refer both to prevailing over something or someone and to the intensification of effort in order to prevail. When I first made that observation twenty years ago, it was in connection with Targumic usage[59] After the completion of my dissertation, Fitzmyer and Harrington published their extremely useful *Manual of Palestinian and Aramaic Texts*.[60] Although the documents in question are largely fragmentary, they established usage in the first century, and the range of meanings of *teqep*, from "taking" through "prevailing" and on to "intensifying," is confirmed there.[61]

What, then, was the meaning of *teqep* in the saying, and why was it rendered differently in Matthew and Luke? Luke's usage is perhaps the simpler to explain: it prevents the association of the kingdom with violence and makes the kingdom's appearance coincident with the activity of the Church. At the same time, the vigor of early Christian preaching (as represented in Acts) actually conveys some of the rougher sense that is more obvious in *teqep*. Matthew's "breaks in violently" (*biazetai* read as middle voice) may also be rendered "suffers violence" (*biazetai* read as passive voice); in either meaning of the Greek form, the context is provided by what follows and determines the significance of the whole. "Violent men take it hostage" may only be understood to refer to the violence directed at preachers of God's kingdom since the time of John.

That last element of the saying (c) has been mediated to Matthew's Gospel through an alternative tradition, which is also represented in the *Gospel of the Nazarenes*.[62] The alternative tradition has the kingdom of

---

59. *God in Strength,* 225-229.

60. See n. 31 above.

61. Because Targum Jonathan, from which I took my examples, was first produced between 70 and 135, the correspondence of usage is not surprising.

62. For a description of the *Gospel of the Nazarenes,* see P. Vielhauer and

God "taken hostage," and then the statement about violent men. In other words, the saying in *Nazarenes* is throughout an indictment of violence against John (and, implicitly, Jesus and his followers). Luke is here a surer guide to the meaning of the saying in "Q": "everyone breaks into it violently." Once more, the flexibility of *teqep* in Aramaic was exploited in the original saying and challenged translators from the beginning of the Gospel traditions.

In order to represent the saying in English, I have suggested using the flexibility of the verb "avail." It derives from the Latin *valere* ("be strong, prevail") and manifests a wide range of meanings in the history of the English language. The *Oxford English Dictionary* lists (among other meanings) "have force," "be of value," "benefit oneself," "make use of," "impose upon," and "give advantage" as senses that have appeared. For that reason, I suggested that the original saying should be rendered:

a) The law and the prophets were until John, from then
b) the kingdom of God avails itself (it has force or imposes itself)
c) and everyone avails himself of it (takes advantage).

The Synoptic Gospels agree in relating a dispute between Jesus and high priests (together with their supporters) concerning Jesus' authority (Matt. 21:23-27; Mark 11:27-33; Luke 20:1-8). That was an issue that Jesus' behavior in the Temple (which we will discuss in the next chapter) made pressing. His reply to his disputants involves an appeal to the authority of John's baptism. Though the material derives from the Petrine source of teaching, the present saying from "Q" is naturally associated with it.

Jesus insisted that John marked the moment from which the kingdom radiated toward all those who were willing to grasp it. The radiance of the kingdom was a matter of its forceful extension and forceful apprehension, divine initiative and human response. The dynamic of that radiance is such that its force, its strength, is Jesus' preoccupation. In the light of the availability of the kingdom, it mattered less to him than it did to others to specify the point from which the kingdom was generated and the horizon to which it was extending.

G. Strecker, "The Gospel of the Nazaraeans," in *New Testament Apocrypha* I: *Gospels and Related Writings*, ed. W. Schneemelcher, tr. R. McL. Wilson (2nd ed., London: SCM, 1991) 154-165. For the reading at issue, which is rendered "is plundered" (another possibility), see *fragment* 8 on p. 160.

Summary

The dynamics of generation and extension were more important to Jesus than whether the kingdom would truly start in Jerusalem and what mix of Jews and righteous non-Jews it would end with. The indeterminacy that we saw in the parable of the mustard seed is not renounced in Jesus' puzzling statement about the available kingdom. Rather, the reason for his indeterminacy becomes plain: Jesus was focused on the dynamics of the kingdom coming in strength[63] to the extent that its location in human terms was secondary. That made for a tension between Jesus and the institutions of his day that will be explored further in the next chapter.

Conclusion: Jesus and the Dynamics of the Kingdom

Jesus' programmatic references to the kingdom of God, transmitted within the earliest cycles of primitive Christian tradition (the Petrine source and "Q") locate him precisely in Judaic discourse. His theology is comparable to that of the Psalms and to those of the Sadducees, the Pharisees, and the Essenes: all had distinctive but comparable understandings of the kingdom of God. The five coordinates of the kingdom that are manifest in Judaic discussion of the kingdom are also obvious in Jesus' authentic sayings. At the same time, a distinctive and characteristic perspective has also emerged in the course of our exegesis.[64]

Eschatology

The kingdom of God was for Jesus a near reality. About to impinge on the world as we know it, the kingdom demanded attention and required announcement. The kingdom exists with the certainty of the immortal

---

63. It is the kingdom "in strength" or "in power" that is the object of the prophets' vision in Mark 9:1 *(en dynamei)*. This is a reflection of the nominal form of *tĕqēp* in Aramaic: *bitqop*. That very form occurs in the Targum of Isaiah, one verse after an innovative reference to the kingdom of God (see Targum of Isaiah 40:9, 10).

64. The present conclusion is not a summary; summaries have been provided at the close of each section.

prophets in the heavenly court, and yet it is to be prayed for. Regular prayer for the kingdom characterizes the eschatology of Jesus. Its coming is not fixed, but that for which one seeks and orders one's life. The eschatological coordinate of the kingdom points one toward the future as the time of ultimate disclosure, and yet resists any calendrical computation.

Transcendence

Because the kingdom has drawn near in time, it may actually touch the world as we know it in space. Jesus casts out demons: the leaven of the kingdom is at work and spreading. The dawning reality that transforms us is both "within you and outside you," as *Thomas* 3 attests. The kingdom is at no one point of generation. It is as available and pervasive as yeast.

Judgment

The impetus to respond to the near and present kingdom changes our routine. The festivities demand readiness and a willingness to put aside duties and wealth for the sake of the feast. The kingdom is a dearer object, a truer wealth, than any other treasure. The ethics of the kingdom are the ethics of possession, of obtaining what is extended to us but that only we can attain.

Purity

Attaining the kingdom is the true vocation of Israel, and Jesus treated all in Israel as suitably clean for that purpose. They are called from east and west to celebrate the kingdom with the patriarchs. With whatever customs of purity they follow, fellowship at meals of the kingdom is open to them. Once one is in Israel and preparing for the kingdom, nothing outside a person defiles one. Defilement is rather a failure to recognize the others of Israel, a refusal to share with the pure Israel that those others represent. Instead of inventing barriers between God's kingdom and his people, Jesus insisted that each person should simply take the kingdom's treasure as a child grabs what it wants. Enthusiastic desire generates a purity fit for the kingdom.

Radiance

The kingdom is as ordinary and miraculous as a mustard seed, and it produces a bounty that the birds have sense enough to make use of, and so should we. The force of the revelation is such that it legitimates a forceful reaction, a vehemence that takes us beyond conventional speech. At the same time, the dynamic of radiance is such that the fact of that extension is of more importance than the definition of who precisely is to be included within it.

The Character of Jesus' Theology

At no point in the authentic sayings of Jesus is there a clear, prosaic description of the kingdom or of the moment or the method of its coming. It is out there in the future, but near, within us and outside us. Jesus himself cast out demons in its name and thereby provided a root of christology, but in his sayings leaven is the kingdom's image as much as he himself is. We are to be ready for what we cannot see and pure by standards Jesus refuses to set. The radiance of the kingdom is there to shelter us, even as we risk all to storm in. Deliberate paradox is obviously part and parcel of Jesus' message.

The place of paradox in Jesus' teaching has been investigated keenly in recent years.[65] Paradox can, of course, be used as an occasion to see things in a new way, to break through habits of thought that are not appropriate to the apprehension of a new reality. But the breakthrough that animated Jesus was not simply cognitive. He understood the kingdom of which he spoke to be final, all-pervading, perfect, holy, and radiant. It was to consume all that is, even as it opened itself to all.

Yet he spoke, not in purely visionary terms, but of the promise of the kingdom in the midst of the ordinary. Although final, the kingdom is also

---

65. See Amos N. Wilder, *Eschatology and Ethics in the Teaching of Jesus* (New York: Harper, 1950); James Breech, *The Silence of Jesus: The Authentic Voice of the Historical Man* (Philadelphia: Fortress, 1983).

near. A host of small disclosures tell of what is to be fully immanent, even as finite acts of love herald the perfect justice that is to be. The ordinary purity of Israel at table is as much a seal of the kingdom's sanctity as a mustard seed is proof of its eventual consummation.

Precisely because Jesus emphasized the ordinary as the medium of the divine, his teaching of the kingdom seems strangely indeterminate. He neither embraces nor challenges the Temple as the center of God's sanctity; he neither accepts nor rejects the Roman Imperium as the legitimate instrument of political power. He will not be pinned down in regard to when the kingdom will be, where it is or will be, what acts precisely will insure one's entry, how purity consistent with the kingdom is to be maintained, or who finally will be able to nest in its shelter. Almost any other Judaic theology of the kingdom will answer those questions more clearly than Jesus does. Only he will turn to the pragmatics of daily living and insist that the kingdom is to be found there.

In Jesus' teaching, the coordinates of the kingdom become the dynamics of the kingdom: the ways in which God is active with his people. Because God as kingdom is active, response to him is active, not merely cognitive. The kingdom of God is a matter of performing the hopeful dynamics of God's revelation to his people. For that reason, Jesus' teaching was not only a matter of making statements, however carefully crafted and remembered. He also engaged in characteristic activities, a conscious performance of the kingdom, which invited Israel to enter into the reality that he also portrayed in words.

Jesus' performance of the kingdom will be the topic of the next chapter, but a final reflection may help us to see why Jesus needed to resist abstract formulations in order to maintain his focus on the kingdom. Because his distinctive theology was that God was revealing himself definitively in the leaven, in the graspings of a child, in his own exorcisms, in the mustard seed, and in the ways we might pray for it and see it, any limitation was inappropriate. He was not explicitly a universalist; had he been, the Church's controversies over circumcision and rules of purity could not have occurred. But Jesus thought so consistently within the terms of reference of what could be seen, heard, or otherwise experienced that the social boundaries of the world outside — Jew and non-Jew, Roman and subject, priest and peasant — receded into the background.

Writing during the third century, Origen, the theologian who resided first in Alexandria and then in Caesarea, denied that God could be described as bodily, although he is the source of all nature and mind, because he is spirit (*On First Principles* 1.2.8).[66] Mystical theology since Origen has described God as a sphere whose center is nowhere and whose circumference is everywhere.[67] The focus on the nature of God's revelation caused Origen to deny both locality and limit in speaking of God. Jesus engaged in a similar distortion of conventional geometry, the usual language of the kingdom, in his insistence on consuming the formulation of boundaries within the details of experience.

Once experience and activity are taken to be the terms of reference of the kingdom, what one actually does is also an instrument of its revelation, an aspect of its radiance. Jesus' awareness of that caused him to act as programmatically as he spoke, to make of his total activity a parable of the kingdom. That, too, was appreciated by Origen, who referred to Jesus as *autobasileia,* the kingdom itself.[68] Jesus, in speaking of his exorcisms, approached that statement himself, although, in his own conception, that made him no better than mustard seed or leaven.

66. See Johannes Quaesten, *Patrology* II (Antwerp: Spectrum, 1953) 75-76.

67. Origen's own expression of the idea appears in his treatise *On Prayer* 23. It is strikingly similar to Plotinus's description of the world-soul in *On Difficulties about the Soul* 4. For the precise phrasing of the theme during the Middle Ages, see Dietrich Mahnke, *Unendliche Sphaere und Allmittelpunkt* (Halle: Niemeyer, 1937).

68. The term appears in his commentary on Matt. 18:23, perhaps as a borrowing from Marcion; see Karl Ludwig Schmidt, "βασιλεία," *Theological Dictionary of the New Testament* I, ed. G. Kittel, tr. G. W. Bromiley (Grand Rapids: Eerdmans, 1978) 579-590, here 589.

CHAPTER 5

Jesus' Activity for
the Kingdom of God

In a recent book, E. P. Sanders has complained that scholars have focused on the sayings of Jesus to the exclusion of study of what Jesus did. Sanders suggests that we concentrate on certain deeds of Jesus that may be regarded as "almost indisputable facts." However much the perspectives of scholars might diverge, the data that they seek to understand and interpret include Jesus' baptism by John, his ministry of preaching and healing within Israel, his calling and sending of disciples, and his confrontation with cultic authorities in the Temple.[1]

The corrective Sanders suggests is pertinent because there has been a tendency to interpret Jesus' teaching as a set of abstract assertions without precise context. Considered in the abstract, Jesus' sayings can be reduced to a few banalities, the supposed religious truth that remains the same through the ages. The discussion above in chapter 1, particularly in relation to symbolist readings of Jesus' position (pp. 16-21), illustrates how problems emerge when sayings are removed from the culture in which they were produced and are transplanted into the environment of what we think of as truth in the present.

By keeping Jesus' practices in mind, as well as his teaching, we keep the issue of cultural context clearly in view. "Deeds" have no meaning apart from the culture in which they are accomplished; they cannot be

---

1. See Sanders, *Jesus and Judaism* (Philadelphia: Fortress, 1985) 3-13.

102

understood in the abstract any more than sayings can be. At the same time, it is important to bear in mind that what a person says is often the best commentary there is on what that person does. We will only understand Jesus historically, in his impact on his followers and on the movement that continued in his name, to the degree that we appreciate both his teaching and his characteristic activity in their original contexts and in relation to one another.

The discussion in the last chapter brought us to the conclusion that Jesus developed a well-articulated and distinctive understanding of the kingdom of God. The challenge that Sanders has rightly issued involves relating Jesus' teaching of the kingdom to what he did, to his public activity. If Jesus focused his attention as keenly on the the kingdom as the sayings we have considered make it seem, then his public activity must have been not merely characteristic but programmatic — a conscious response to the claim that *God* made as true king.

Many of the "almost indisputable facts" that Sanders lists might have been applied to some other rabbi within Jesus' period. Teaching, healing, and calling disciples were typical activities among the rabbis. Not every rabbi was noted for all three activities, but in aggregate rabbis were known to be active in those ways. In addition, rabbis were especially reputed for their expertise in adjudicating matters of purity. "Purity" is not on Sanders's list, but there is practically no dispute that Jesus engaged in discussion and controversy concerning purity (as has been considered in the last chapter, pp. 80-90). In all these aspects, then, Jesus presents a typically rabbinic profile.[2]

The reference to Jesus as a rabbi can easily cause confusion, because the dominant movement that we know of as Rabbinic Judaism did not emerge until after 70 CE. The destruction of the Temple and the resulting displacement of high-priestly authority created a vacuum of power. Local sages and teachers, who had previously been engaged in issues of purity and conduct, stepped into the breach, and organized themselves in centers of learning in cities such as Sepphoris and Tiberias. The rabbis who had been local and rural sages before 70 CE increasingly became formally trained Rabbis after 70 CE, hierarchical and metropolitan authorities who attempted to formulate what it meant to be Israel. Rabbinic literature only emerged, beginning with the publication of the

---

2. For a useful introduction, see Jacob Neusner, *Judaism in the Beginning of Christianity* (Philadelphia: Fortress, 1988).

Mishnah in 200 CE, as a result of the mature development of Rabbinic Judaism.[3]

The term "rabbi" was used in relation to teachers before 70 CE. Joshua ben Peradija (who lived ca. 104-78 BCE) was known by that title according to the Mishnah (see *Aboth* 1:6 and also 1:16). An ossuary from Jesus' period also attests the usage.[4] In a culture that respects learning, it is only to be expected that a student might address a respected teacher as "great," which is what *rab* means. When I call a teacher "great," I indicate that I defer to him; he is greater than I am in the expertise that is involved. That relational understanding becomes emphatic in the form *rabbi*, "my great one." In the book of Daniel, Daniel himself is named "*rab* of the prefects of the wise" by King Nebuchadnezzar (Dan. 2:48; see also 4:6; 5:11). In the Aramaic usage involved, the natural way for one of those beneath Daniel to address him would have been as "rabbi."

Jesus is addressed in the Gospels as "rabbi" more often than with any other designation; it is obviously what his followers called him (Matt. 26:25, 49; Mark 9:5; 10:51; 11:21; 14:45; John 1:38, 49; 3:2; 4:31; 6:25; 9:2; 11:8). The designation comports well with his characteristic activities, especially his adjudications regarding purity and his public dispute with the authorities in the Temple. When twentieth-century scholars have expressed reservations about referring to Jesus as a rabbi, they have had in mind the danger of identifying Jesus with the post-70 CE Rabbinic movement, which was more systematized than the teachings of rabbis before that time and which amounted to the established power within Judaism.

Unfortunately, anxiety in respect of that anachronism can result in the far greater error of placing Jesus within "sectarian" Judaism. The early Judaism of Jesus' time was so pluralistic that the dichotomy between "orthodox" and "sectarian" forms of the religion is not helpful. Worse still, denying Jesus the address of rabbi, which his first followers used of him, can be part of an attempt to separate him from Judaism. The most famous recent attempt is that of John Dominic Crossan, who would make Jesus into one of the "Cynic" philosophers whom Crossan

3. See Chilton, "Rabbinic Traditions and Writings," in *Dictionary of Jesus and the Gospels*, ed. J. B. Green, S. McKnight, and I. H. Marshall (Downers Grove: InterVarsity, 1992) 651-660. As is explained in that article, some local sages were "Pharisees," but many were not.

4. See J. P. Kane, "Ossuary Inscriptions of Jerusalem," *Journal of Semitic Studies* 23 (1978) 268-282.

styles as "hippies in a world of Augustan yuppies." The argument can only be maintained by ignoring the cultural context of the Gospels and by an extremely elastic understanding of what a "Cynic" might have been.[5] That Jesus was a teacher from Galilee, a rabbi from peasantry, is a finding in which Sanders and I completely agree.[6]

Once Jesus is understood as a local sage, some of his behavior is easily explained. Teaching, calling disciples to learn from one's example, discussing issues of purity, even healing, all belong to the general category of what such a teacher might be expected to do. We might compare Jesus to two of his most famous near contemporaries, Ḥanina ben Dosa and Hillel.

Ḥanina is said in the Talmud (*Berakhoth* 34b) to have prayed successfully for healing at a distance in a story that is very similar to Matt. 8:5-13; Luke 7:1-10; and John 4:46-53.[7] Both Ḥanina and Jesus are said to receive a request from a person concerning that person's child or servant. (In Luke and Berakhoth emissaries make the request; the father or master appears in person in Matthew and John.) Both Ḥanina and Jesus have the prayerful insight to know that healing has been achieved, and the child or servant is indeed healed from the time that each rabbi said so. There are fascinating differences among the stories, but they cannot be treated here; neither can we settle here the question of the historical reliability of the stories. The cultural similarity between the *memory* of Ḥanina and the *memory* of Jesus is our present concern. In each case, a rabbi is said to have been involved in healing.

Ḥanina lived during the first century, but after the death of Jesus. Hillel, on the other hand, was a slightly older contemporary of Jesus. The Talmud tells the story that Hillel was once approached by a man who wanted to convert to Judaism; but the man wished to be taught

5. Crossan's views are discussed in Chilton, "Jesus within Judaism," in *Judaism in Late Antiquity* 2, ed. J. Neusner (Handbuch der Orientalistik 17; Leiden: Brill, 1995) 262-284. Crossan's principal publication is *The Historical Jesus: The Life of a Mediterranean Jewish Peasant* (San Francisco: Harper/Edinburgh: Clark, 1991); see pp. 421 and 422 for his position as cited here.

6. Cf. my *A Galilean Rabbi and His Bible: Jesus' Use of the Interpreted Scripture of His Time* (Wilmington: Glazier, 1984), also published with the subtitle *Jesus' Own Interpretation of Isaiah* (London: SPCK, 1984).

7. See the treatment in George Foot Moore, *Judaism in the First Centuries of the Christian Era: The Age of the Tannaim* 1 (Cambridge: Harvard University Press, 1927) 377-378. The comparison was popularized in Geza Vermes, *Jesus the Jew: A Historian's Reading of the Gospels* (Philadelphia: Fortress, 1986) 74-75.

the Torah quickly, while he stood on one foot. Hillel told him: "That which you hate, do not do to your neighbor. That is the whole Torah, while everything else is commentary: go and learn it!" (see *Shabbath* 31a). Jesus' teaching concerning the principle of love in the Torah is an obvious analogy (see Matt. 22:34-40; Mark 12:28-34; Luke 10:25-26).

Whether viewed from the perspective of prayer and healing (as in the case of Ḥanina) or from the perspective of teaching and thought (as in the case of Hillel), Jesus appears to have been comparable to his rabbinic colleagues. Such a comparison may be pursued along other lines.[8] But comparison is never fruitful if it becomes a form of simplistic reduction. To say simply that Jesus was a rabbi is no more informative than saying that Hillel and Ḥanina were rabbis, that Caiaphas was a priest, or that Pilate was a Roman prefect. All such statements represent no more than points of departure in historical description. They refer to categories that are inadequate to convey just who these people were, although they do provide an indication of the social fields in which these people were active.

Once we appreciate the field within which a person's memory was preserved, we are in a position to analyze what makes that memory distinctive. Hillel's skill in oral tradition, Ḥanina's repute as a thauma-turge, Caiaphas's acquiescence to Roman administration in Jerusalem, and Pilate's tendency to bait the Jews,[9] all become apparent when they are studied and compared to those with whom they are generally similar, and yet from whom they are strikingly different. The same principle applies in the study of the memory of Jesus in the Gospels.

Much of what Jesus is remembered to have done and said comports well with rabbinic activity: the concern for purity and ablutions (a concern that included the practice of baptism), the programmatic emphasis on teaching and healing, the development of characteristic themes in his teaching (such as "the kingdom of God"), the gathering of disciples for whom that teaching was presented in a repeatable form or *mishnah* (a noun that derives from the verb *shanah*, "to repeat"). Most of the passages that present Jesus in dispute with his Pharisaic, scribal, and priestly

8. In addition to the books by Moore and Vermes which have already been cited, see David Flusser, *Die rabbinische Gleichnisse und der Gleichniserzähler Jesus* (Judaica et Christiana 4; Las Vegas: Lang, 1981) and my *A Galilean Rabbi and His Bible*.

9. The relevant data concerning Caiaphas and Pilate are discussed in my *The Temple of Jesus: His Sacrificial Program within a Cultural History of Sacrifice* (University Park: Pennsylvania State University, 1992) 91-111.

contemporaries are also in line with some of the vigorous arguments one encounters in Rabbinic literature. In all of those aspects, Jesus' activity seems broadly similar to what might have been expected of a rabbi.

Within that broad similarly, however, two strong aspects of distinctiveness appear. First, Jesus is remembered, not only to have gathered disciples, but to have sent out twelve of them in order to teach and to act in his name. The correspondence between the number of disciples commissioned to do so and the scriptural number of the tribes of Israel reinforces the impression that Jesus sent the twelve as a consciously distinctive act.[10]

Second, although rabbinic controversies in the Temple could result in disorder, violence, and even bloodshed,[11] Jesus' controversy in the Temple, involving both his occupation of the great outer court and ultimately his execution at the order of Pilate, stands out as an unusual confrontation between a rabbi's authority and the priestly authority in the Temple, which had been underwritten by Rome. No historical description of Jesus can claim to be adequate that fails to explain the causes of that fateful confrontation, because that is just where he becomes a figure whom history has not forgotten. However memorable Jesus' teaching may have been on its own merits, it was his crucifixion as a result of his occupation of the Temple that became the centerpiece of the Gospels and of the movement that came to called "Christian."

The purpose of this chapter is therefore to investigate Jesus' sending of the twelve disciples and his occupation of the Temple in the context of how he spoke of the kingdom of God. Were those actions related to the kingdom in his thinking? If so, how was that relationship realized, and what does it suggest for our understanding of the underlying concept of the kingdom?

Jesus' Sending of the Twelve

Recent discussion of the source known as "Q" has brought about a remarkable consensus that at least some of the sayings within it were

10. For a brilliant discussion of the question, see Ben F. Meyer, *The Aims of Jesus* (London: SCM, 1979) 153-154.

11. For examples, see *The Temple of Jesus,* 101-103, 183.

circulated a few years after the crucifixion, around the year 35 CE. A recent study includes in the earliest version of "Q" a charge to Jesus' disciples (Luke 10:3-6, 9-11, 16), a strategy to cope with resistance to their message (Luke 6:27-35), examples of how to speak of the kingdom (Luke 6:20b-21; 11:2-4, 14-20; 13:18-21), curses to lay on those who reject those sent in the name of the kingdom (Luke 11:39-48, 52), and a section relating John the baptist and Jesus as principal emissaries of the kingdom (Luke 7:24b-26, 28a, 33-34).[12]

The reconstruction proposed by Leif Vaage follows in the wake of the recent fashion of proposing multiple versions of Q prior to the composition of Matthew and Luke. He cites John Kloppenborg's hypothesis of three redactions of Q prior to the Gospels, but in his own analysis his concern is to distinguish the formative stage from the redaction more generally. In that approach, Vaage's work is comparable to the more conservative contribution of David Catchpole, which appeared in the previous year.[13]

Catchpole isolates the formative material of the charge to Jesus' disciples much as Vaage does (Luke 10:3, 4, 5-7, 9, 10a, 11a, 12). He sees it as "an integrated whole stemming from Jesus himself" that has been layered over with additional material (Luke 10:2, 13-15, 16). The additional material represents the especial concerns of Q: christology, eschatology, and the final mission to Israel on Jesus' behalf.[14]

The agreement between Vaage and Catchpole in regard to the formative stage of Q makes their profound disagreement in regard to the cultural milieu of Q all the more striking. According to Vaage (p. 106), "Like the Cynics, the 'Galilean upstarts' whom Q's formative stratum represents conducted in word and deed a form of 'popular' resistance to the official truths and virtues of their day." Catchpole sees, on the other hand (p. 188), "a preoccupation with a mission to Israel,

---

12. See Leif E. Vaage, *Galilean Upstarts: Jesus' First Followers According to Q* (Valley Forge: Trinity Press International, 1994). He defends his choice of the material at the formative stage of Q in agreement with the recent work of John S. Kloppenborg, Vaage, pp. 107-120. Since the time of Adolf von Harnack, there has been a lively discussion of whether Matthew or Luke more accurately represents Q. Harnack sided with Matthew; see *The Sayings of Jesus*, tr. J. R. Wilkinson (New York: Putnam, 1908) 172-182. Vaage follows the current fashion in preferring Luke and in citing Q according to chapter and verse in Luke.

13. *The Quest for Q* (Edinburgh: Clark, 1993).

14. *The Quest for Q*, 188.

which needs to be expanded by means of yet more charismatically endowed missionaries sent out by a settled but charismatic community with the authority of God himself." The opposition of these positions is even greater than may appear at first reading: while Vaage is characterizing the earliest stage of Q, Catchpole is speaking of the redactional product.

Both of these perspectives are too rigid and distort a critical reading of Q. Vaage relies extensively and unreflectively on Crossan's work, which we have already found inconsistent with the best evidence there is of Jesus' activity (pp. 104-105 above). Catchpole understands the "confrontational sense"[15] of such statements as John the baptist's claim that God could raise up children for Abraham from stones in order to replace those of Israel who refused to repent (Luke 3:8); but he does not adequately allow for the distance from Israel such a threat implies.

Q is better seen as evolving in two distinct stages. In the first, Jesus' teaching was arranged in the form of a mishnah by his disciples. They took up a ministry in Jesus' name that was addressed to Israel at large after the resurrection. The mishnaic form of Q was preserved orally in Aramaic and explained how the twelve were to discharge their mission. It included just the materials that have already been specified: instructions to Jesus' disciples, a strategy of love to overcome resistance, paradigms to illustrate the kingdom, threats directed toward enemies, and a reference to John the baptist that would serve as a transition to baptism in the name of Jesus.[16] As specified, that is probably the original, mishnaic order of Q. It is the order that accords with Q's purpose within the mission to Israel.

At the final stage, Q's order was changed to become quasi-biographical in accordance with the order of the Petrine teaching (see pp. 65-66 above). At that stage, for example, material concerning John the baptist was moved to the beginning, and the story of Jesus' temptations (Luke 4:1-13) was added in order to make the transition to an unequivocal focus on Jesus rather than John. The final redaction of Q probably took place a decade after the mishnaic stage of Q was

15. *The Quest for Q,* 77. On p. 248, the passage is classed with John's prophetic preaching.

16. It seems likely to me, in addition, that Q also preserved at least one saying in reference to eucharist (Luke 22:15). See Chilton, *A Feast of Meanings: Eucharistic Theologies from Jesus through Johannine Circles* (Supplements to *Novum Testamentum* 72; Leiden: Brill, 1994) 72-74, 94-96.

composed, probably in Syria, an environment in which both Aramaic and Greek were spoken.[17]

Catchpole and Vaage are both competent guides in the attempt to understand Luke 10:1-12, the commission of the seventy or seventy-two disciples (the number varying in the manuscripts). Catchpole adduces much Rabbinic material to elucidate the text, while Vaage cites a range of Cynic sources. Both analogies are helpful in understanding the literary shape of the commission, but the focus here is different. Our purpose is to understand the commission of the disciples in terms of the kingdom, and the kingdom in terms of the commission. If, as seems to be the case, Q in its mishnaic phase represents Jesus' charge to his disciples as he sent them out to be his representatives, it should reflect his own programmatic activity more lucidly than any inference that we might draw regarding his intentions. Jesus' commission is the closest thing there is to his own commentary on his actions.

What the disciples are told to do seems strange unless the image of the harvest at the beginning of the charge (Luke 10:2) is taken seriously.[18] Because they are going out as to rich fields, they do not require what would normally be required on a journey: purse, bag, and sandals are dispensed with. Their charge is to treat Israel as a field in which one works, not as an itinerary of travel; greeting people along the way (which would only lead to diversions from the task) is even proscribed (v. 4).

In addition, staffs are also prohibited, although they were normally used on journeys for support and protection. That is a detail that we actually know from Luke 9:3, the commission of the twelve (rather than the seventy). Luke 9:3 also prohibits carrying a bag, a provision of bread, money, or a change of clothing. Matt. 10:9-10 agrees in regard to money, bag, clothing, sandals, and staff, but does not prohibit bread. Mark 6:8-9 prohibits bread, bag, and money, but both a staff and sandals are positively prescribed!

---

17. See Siegfried Schulz, Q. Die Spruchquelle der Evangelisten (Zurich: Theologischer Verlag, 1972). It should be mentioned that there is an extensive bibliography on Q, reaching back over two centuries (and much of it in German). The impression is sometimes given in North America that the hypothesis is new; in fact, it is an old and well-founded theory.

18. In this regard, I agree with Kloppenborg against Vaage; see Vaage, pp. 107-108; John S. Kloppenborg, The Formation of Q (Philadelphia: Fortress, 1987) 193, 200. The metaphor of the harvest is also applied to discipleship by Rabbi Tarfon in Aboth 2:15.

All those additional privations comport with the command to go without sandals and were a part of the original charge. Each Gospel softens the stringent requirements somewhat. Matthew omits the prohibition of bread, and Luke divides the prohibitions between the twelve (9:1-6) and the seventy (10:1-12). In a more radical way, Mark 6:9 turns the prohibition of sandals into a command to wear them. By the same transformation, Mark 6:8 specifies that a staff "alone" *should* be carried, so that the imagery of discipleship shifts from treating all Israel as one's household to passing through territory that might prove hostile. Such variations reflect differences in primitive Christian practice and in conceptions of discipleship. Similarly, the number of disciples in Luke 10:1, seventy or seventy-two, accommodates to the traditional number of the nations of the world, while the earlier figure of twelve in Matt. 10:5 and Mark 6:7 represents both the intention of Jesus to address all Israel and the mishnaic stage of Q. The image of Israel as a field ripe for harvest dominates the details of the charge to the disciples in the earliest form of the commission, Jesus' mishnah.

Another, powerful analogy is at work within the commission. The Mishnah reflects the common practice in Jerusalem of prohibiting pilgrims from entering the Temple with the bags and staffs and purses that they had traveled with (*Berakhoth* 9:5).[19] All such items were to be deposited prior to worship so that one was present simply as a representative of Israel. Part of worship was that one was to appear in one's simple purity. The issue of purity also features prominently in the charge to the disciples (although it is overlooked far too often).

The very next injunction (Luke 10:5-8) instructs the disciples to offer their peace to any house of a village they enter. They are to accept hospitality in that house, eating what is set before them. The emphasis on eating what is provided is repeated (Luke 10:7, 8), so that it does not appear to be a later marginal elaboration.[20] In Pharisaic constructions of purity as they are reflected in the Mishnah, the foods one ate and the hospitality one offered and accepted were carefully regulated. In the tractate *Demai* (2:2), which concerns tithing, one who undertakes to be

---

19. See *The Temple of Jesus*, 100-111.

20. Catchpole may be correct in stating that the form of 10:8 is redactional, from the time of the composition of the Gospel (pp. 176-178). But he is also correct in assigning 10:7 to Q (pp. 184-185), and that is where the motif first appears, within the ministry of Jesus.

faithful must tithe what he eats, what he sells, and what he buys, *and not accept hospitality from any "person of the land"* ('*am ha-'ares*, "person of the land," is a phrase used since Zech. 7:5 of those whose practices in tithing and other matters could not be trusted). *Demai* further specifies (2:3) that a faithful person must not sell wet or dry produce to a person of the land and must not buy wet produce from him, since wet produce was held to be more susceptible to uncleanness. The passage goes on to make the rule against hospitality reciprocal: one cannot have a person of land as a guest when that person is wearing his own (probably impure) garments; the guest must must first change his clothing. These strictures clearly reflect a construction of purity among the "faithful" (the *haberim*) that sets them apart from other Jews by restrictions on the food one might eat and trade and the commerce and fellowship one might enjoy.[21]

Jesus' insistence that his disciples accept hospitality in whatever house would accept them is fully consonant with his reputation as "a glutton and a drunkard" (Matt. 11:19 and Luke 7:34, discussed on pp. 80 and 83). There is a deliberate carelessness involved, in the precise sense that the disciples are not to have a care in regard to the practices of purity of those who offer hospitality to them. They are true Israelites. When they join in the meals of the kingdom and when they accept and grant forgiveness to one another in the manner of the Lord's Prayer, what they set on the table of fellowship from their own effort is by definition pure and should be gratefully consumed. The twelve disciples define and create the true Israel to which they are sent, and they tread that territory as on holy ground, shoeless, without staff or purse.

The activities of the disciples in the fellowship of Israel are essentially to be the activities of Jesus. As Luke presents Q, they are to heal the sick and preach that the kingdom has drawn near (Luke 10:9); as Matthew presents Q, they are to preach that the kingdom has drawn near and heal, they are to raise the dead, cleanse lepers, and caste out demons, all the while taking and giving freely (Matt. 10:7-8). Catchpole observes that the wording of Matthew correlates the disciples' activities with Jesus' activities, and he thinks the correlation was introduced when the Gospel was composed.[22] But the correlation involved is with mate-

---

21. For a discussion of the passage as a reflection of practice in the first century, see *A Feast of Meanings*, 165-166.
22. *The Quest for Q*, p. 167.

rial in Q: Jesus' statement of what John the baptist should be told that Jesus himself is doing (Matt. 11:5 and Luke 7:22). For that reason, Matthew at this point may be held to represent the more primitive wording. In any case, the coordination of the disciples' activity with that of Jesus is manifestly an organic aspect of the charge in Q.

The extent of the identity between what Jesus does and what the disciples do is clearly represented at the close of the charge, where the disciples are instructed to shake the dust off their feet from any place that does not receive them (Luke 10:11). That gesture is, of course, vivid on any reading. But on the understanding of the charge that we have developed here, the symbolism is particularly acute. Towns that do not receive the disciples have cut themselves off from the kingdom of God and can expect worse than what is in store for Sodom (vv. 11-12).[23] The disciples treat them as impure on Jesus' personal authority.

Taken as a whole, Jesus' charge to the disciples at the mishnaic stage of Q is an enacted parable of the kingdom of God. The coordinates of the kingdom that have been explored in the previous chapter are here put into action. In the cases of four of the five coordinates of the kingdom, the link between the action prescribed here and the sayings of Jesus is explicit.

That the kingdom has drawn near is the foundation of everything that is commanded, and the disciples are to address the people they gather in towns and villages in order to announce that dawning reality. Their preaching is in itself a witness to the nature of Jesus' eschatology. Likewise, their engagement in a ministry of healing attests to the immanence of the kingdom. The strong man of ailment is bound in order that the stronger man of the kingdom might prevail (Matt. 12:28-29; Mark 3:27; Luke 11:20-22). That triumphant immanence of the kingdom, whether marked by healing or by the wider range of victories indicated in Matt. 10:8 (compare Luke 10:9), appears in the context of purity. The purity of the kingdom is such as to accept that each forgiven and forgiving Israelite is clean in himself and clean in what he produces. Much of the charge to the disciples is arranged to emphasize the un-

---

23. The explicit reference to the kingdom in Luke 10:11 is attributed by Catchpole (p. 185) to the stage of the redaction of the Gospel, although he admits that the actual form of words is nearer to Q's than is Luke 10:9 (p. 164). This is a rare case of self-contradiction, and in this case his judgment should not be accepted. Vaage, on the other hand, would excise 10:12 from Q's formative stage (p. 108): his Cynic Jesus can simply have nothing to do with judgment.

derstanding of purity that enables the triumphant immanence of the kingdom. Rejection of that kingdom, in the shape of its emissaries, can by itself render the very dust of the town unclean. Accepting or rejecting the kingdom is the sole ground on which judgment ultimately is conducted.

The last coordinate of the kingdom in Jesus' teaching, the coordinate of radiance, remains largely unaddressed by the charge to the disciples. It is evident that a certain progression from the commissioned disciples to those they lodge with is presupposed, and the decision to treat all Israel as pure attests to the conviction that the radiant power of the kingdom is effecting a change. But those effects are corollaries of a larger conception that is not spelled out here: where is the kingdom starting from, and how — and in what directions — is it extending itself?

The sayings treated in the last chapter (pp. 91-97) provide answers to such questions only in terms of the dynamic of the kingdom's radiance. The parable of the mustard seed (Matt. 13:31-32; Mark 4:30-32; Luke 13:18-19; *Thomas* 20) refers to the extension of the kingdom from any center, any point of its revelation. The characterization of the violent availability of the kingdom (Matt. 11:12; Luke 16:16) insists on the radical apprehension of the kingdom, wherever it is revealed. But neither saying identifies a reliable place or institution from which the kingdom comes; neither defines the horizon toward which the kingdom is stretching. The charge of the disciples is consistent with Jesus' ambiguity or indecision in regard to the radiance of the kingdom.

The heightening of this aspect of uncertainty occurs in a context that, for the most part, clarifies and specifies Jesus' conception of the kingdom. Sending the disciples to announce the kingdom as promise (Luke 10:9) and as judgment (v. 11) establishes that Jesus' eschatology is of an ultimate future that impinges on the present. Their ministry of healing warrants the dynamic, transforming immanence of that which finally must be all in all (v. 9). What they teach, in its finality, amounts to a standard according to which hearers will be judged (vv. 10-12). And they enact the generic purity of Israel, which is the presupposition of the kingdom's revelation (vv. 5-8).

In the Gospel according to John, Jesus' brothers taunt him for not going to Jerusalem for the feast of Sukkoth (Tabernacles). They say to him, "No one acts in secret and seeks himself to be in the open. If you do these things, show yourself to the world" (John 7:4). The idiom of the Gospel at this point is thoroughly christological, in that the concern is with Jesus' identity. But the question may well be asked in the idiom of the kingdom (and may originally have been asked in that way): if the kingdom is upon us and immanent, the standard of final judgment and the index of purity, then what is its public point of manifestation? How can all that Jesus says in parable and in action be true, how can the extension of his ministry by his disciples be valid, unless somewhere the kingdom is in the open, a matter of how public Israel radiates its truth to the world?

That urgent issue, as we will see in the next section, is what brought Jesus to Jerusalem and to the cross.

Jesus' Occupation of the Temple

Critical discussion of Jesus, all through the modern period, has been stumped by one, crucial historical question. Anyone who has read the Gospels knows that Jesus was a skilled teacher, a *rabbi* in the sense already described (pp. 103-107 above). He skillfully wove a portrait of God as a divine ruler ("the kingdom of God," in Jesus' words) together with an appeal to people to behave as God's children (by loving both their divine father and their neighbor). At the same time, it is plain that Jesus appeared to be a threat to both Jewish and Roman authorities in Jerusalem. Otherwise he would not have been crucified. The question that has nagged critical discussion concerns the relationship between Jesus the rabbi and Jesus the criminal: how does a teacher of God's ways and God's love find himself on a cross?

The critical pictures of Jesus that have been developed during the past two hundred years portray him as either an appealing, gifted teacher or a vehement political revolutionary. Both kinds of portrait are wanting. If Jesus' teaching were purely abstract, a matter of defining God's nature and the appropriate human response to God, it would be hard to explain why he would invest himself in argument in Jerusalem and why the local aristocracy there would turn against him. On the other hand, if Jesus' purpose was to encourage some sort of rebellion against Rome, why did he devote so much of his ministry to telling memorable parables in Galilee? It is easy enough to imagine Jesus the rabbi *or* Jesus the revolutionary. But how can we do justice to *both* aspects and discover Jesus, the radical rabbi of the first century?

The Gospels all relate an incident that sheds light in this dark corner of modern study (Matt. 21:12-16; Mark 11:15-18; Luke 19:45-48; John 2:14-22). In the passage traditionally called "The Cleansing of the Temple," Jesus boldly enters the holy place where sacrifice was conducted and throws out the people who were converting the currency of Rome into money that was acceptable to the priestly authorities. Such an action would arouse opposition from both the Roman authorities and the priests. The priests would be threatened because an important source of revenue was jeopardized. The Romans would be concerned because they wanted to protect the operation of the Temple, which they saw as a symbol of their tolerant acceptance of Jews as loyal subjects.

The conventional picture of Jesus as preventing commercial activity in God's house is appealing. It enables us to conceive of Jesus as transcending Jewish worship, and that is what the Gospels intend by the story. They are all written with hindsight, in the period after the Temple was destroyed (in 70 CE), when Christianity was emerging as a largely non-Jewish movement. From the early theologians of Christianity to the most modern commentaries, the alluring simplicity of the righteous, philosophical Jesus casting out the "money changers" has proven itself again and again.

As is often the case, the conventional picture of Jesus may only be sustained by ignoring the social realities of early Judaism. There were indeed "money changers" associated with the Temple, whose activities are set down in the Mishnah. Every year, the changing of money — in order to collect the tax of a half shekel from every adult Jewish male — went on publicly throughout Israel. The process commenced a full month before Passover, with a proclamation concerning the tax (Mishnah *Shekalim* 1:1), and exchanges were set up outside Jerusalem ten days *before* they were set up in the Temple (*Shekalim* 1:3). According to Josephus, the tax was not even limited to those resident in the land of Israel (*War* 7.218; *Antiquities* 18.312), but was collected from Jews far and wide. An awareness of those simple facts brings us to an equally simple conclusion: the Gospels' picture of Jesus is distorted. It is clear that he could not have stopped the collection of the half shekel by overturning some tables in the Temple.

A generation after Jesus' death, by the time the Gospels were written, the Temple in Jerusalem had been destroyed and the most influential centers of Christianity were in cities of the Mediterranean world such as Alexandria, Antioch, Corinth, Damascus, Ephesus, and

Rome. There were still large numbers of Jews who were also followers of Jesus, but non-Jews came to predominate in the primitive Church. They had control over how the Gospels were written after 70 CE and how the texts were interpreted. The Synoptic Gospels were composed by one group of teachers after another during the period between Jesus' death and 95 CE. There is a reasonable degree of consensus that Mark was the first of the Gospels to be written, around 71 CE in the environs of Rome. As convention has it, Matthew was subsequently composed, near 80 CE, perhaps in Damascus (or elsewhere in Syria), while Luke came later, say in 90 CE, perhaps in Antioch. Some of the earliest teachers who shaped the Gospels shared the cultural milieu of Jesus, but many had never seen him; they lived far from his land at a later period and were not practicing Jews. John's Gospel was composed in Ephesus around 100 CE and is a reflection on the significance of Jesus for Christians who had the benefit of the sort of teaching that the Synoptic Gospels represent.

The growth of Christianity involved a rapid transition from culture to culture and, within each culture, from subculture to subculture. A basic prerequisite for understanding any text of the Gospels, therefore, is to define the cultural context of a given statement. The cultural context of the picture of Jesus throwing money changers out of the Temple is that of the predominantly non-Jewish audience of the Gospels, who regarded Judaism as a thing of the past, and its worship as corrupt. To attempt seriously to imagine Jesus behaving in that fashion only distorts our understanding of his purposes and encourages the anti-Semitism of Christians. Insensitivity to the cultural milieux of the Gospels goes hand in hand with a prejudicial treatment of cultures other than our own.

Jesus probably *did* object to the tax of a half shekel, as Matt. 17:24-27 indicates. For him, being a child of God (a "son," as he put it) implied that one was free of any imposed payment for the worship of the Temple.[24] But a single onslaught of the sort described in the Gospels would not have amounted to an effective protest against the payment. To stop the collection would have required an assault on the central

---

24. For a fuller discussion, see B. Chilton, "A Coin of Three Realms (Matt. 17.24-27," in *The Bible in Three Dimensions: Essays in Celebration of Forty Years of Biblical Studies in the University of Sheffield,* ed. D. J. A. Clines, S. E. Fowl, and S. E. Porter (*Journal for the Study of the Old Testament* Supplement Series 87; Sheffield: JSOT, 1990) 269-282.

treasuries of the Temple, as well as local treasuries in Israel and beyond. There is no indication that Jesus and his followers attempted anything of the kind, and any action approaching such dimensions would have invited immediate and forceful repression by both Jewish and Roman authorities. There is no evidence that they reacted in that manner to Jesus and his followers.

But Jesus' action in the Temple as attested in the Gospels is not simply a matter of preventing the collection of the half shekel. In fact, Luke 19:45-46 says nothing whatever about "money changers"; because Luke's Gospel is in some ways the most sensitive to historical concerns in the New Testament, the omission seems significant. Luke joins the other Gospels in portraying Jesus' act in the Temple as an occupation designed to prevent the sacrifice of animals that were acquired on the site. The trading involved commerce inside the Temple, and the Jesus of the canonical Gospels, like the Jesus of the *Gospel according to Thomas,* held that "Traders and merchants shall not enter the places of my father" (*Thomas* 64).

Jesus' action in the Temple, understood as a means of asserting the sanctity of the Temple, is comparable to the actions of other Jewish teachers of his period. Josephus reports that the Pharisees made known their displeasure at a high priest (Alexander Jannaeus) by inciting a crowd to pelt him with lemons (at hand for a festal procession) at a time when he should have been promising to offer sacrifice (*Antiquities* 13.372, 373). Josephus also recounts the execution of the rabbis who were implicated in a plot to dismantle the eagle Herod had erected over a gate of the Temple (*War* 1.648-655; *Antiquities* 17.149-167). By comparison, Jesus' action seems almost tame; after all, what he did was expel some vendors, an act less directly threatening to priestly and secular authorities than what some earlier Pharisees had done.

Once it is appreciated that Jesus' maneuver in the Temple was in the nature of a claim on territory in order to eject those performing an activity he obviously disapproved of, it seems more straightforward to characterize it as an "occupation" rather than a "demonstration"; the traditional "cleansing" is obviously an apologetic designation. The purpose of Jesus activity makes good sense in the context of what we know of the activities of other early rabbinic teachers. Hillel was an older contemporary of Jesus who taught (according to Babylonian Talmud *Shabbath* 31) a form of what is known in Christian circles as the Golden Rule taught by Jesus, that we should do to others as we would have them do to us (see pp. 105-106 above). Hillel is also reported to have taught that offerings brought to the Temple should have hands laid on them by their owners and then be given over to priests for slaughter. Recent studies of the anthropology of sacrifice show why such stipulations were held to be important. Hillel was insisting that when the people of Israel came to worship they should offer something from their own property. Putting one's hands on the animal that was about to be sacrificed was a statement of ownership.[25]

The followers of a rabbi named Shammai are typically depicted in Rabbinic literature as resisting the teachings of Hillel. Here, too, they take the part of the opposition. They insist that animals for sacrifice might be given *directly* to priests for slaughter; Hillel's requirement of laying hands on the sacrifice is held to be dispensable. But one of Shammai's followers was so struck by the rectitude of Hillel's position that he had some three thousand animals brought into the Temple and gave them to those who were willing to lay hands on them in advance of sacrifice (Babylonian Talmud *Beṣah* 20a, b; Tosephta *Ḥagigah* 2.11; Jerusalem Talmud *Ḥagigah* 2.3; and *Beṣah* 2.4).[26]

In one sense, the tradition concerning Hillel envisages the opposite movement from what is represented in the tradition concerning Jesus: animals are driven into the Temple, rather than their traders expelled. Yet the purpose of the action by Hillel's partisan is to enforce a certain understanding of correct offering, one that accords with a standard feature of sacrifice in the anthropological literature. Hillel's *halakhah*, in effect, insists on the participation of the offerer by virtue of his ownership of what is offered, while most of the followers of Shammai are portrayed as sanctioning sacrifice more as a self-contained priestly action.

Jesus' occupation of the Temple is best seen — along lines similar to those involved in the provision of animals to support Hillel's position — as an attempt to insist that the offerer's actual ownership of what is offered is a vital aspect of sacrifice. Neither Hillel nor Jesus needs to be understood as acting on any symbolic agenda other than his conception

---

25. For a discussion of the significance of Jesus' occupation of the Temple within an anthropological understanding of sacrifice, see *The Temple of Jesus*.

26. The importance of such disputes in the evaluation of early Judaism is stressed in Martin Hengel and Roland Deines, " 'Common Judaism,' Jesus, and the Pharisees: A Review Article," *Journal of Theological Studies* 46 (1995) 1-70, here 39-41.

of acceptable sacrifice or as appearing to his contemporaries to be anything other than a typical Pharisee, impassioned with purity in the Temple to the point of forceful intervention. Neither of their positions may be understood as a concern with the physical acceptability of the animals at issue. In each case, the question of purity is: What is to be done with what is taken to be clean?

Jesus' occupation of the Temple took place in the context of a particular dispute involving the Pharisees, a controversy over where the action of acquiring animals for sacrifice was to occur. In that the dispute was intimately involved with the issue of how animals were to be procured, it manifests a focus on purity that is akin to that attributed to Hillel and Jesus.

The nature and intensity of the dispute are only comprehensible when the geography of the Temple and its sacrificial function are kept in mind. In the holy of holies, enclosed in a house and beyond a veil, the God of Israel was held to be enthroned in a virtually empty room. Only the high priest could enter that space, and then only once a year, on the Day of Atonement; at the autumnal equinox the rays of the sun could enter the earthly chamber whence the sun's ruler exercised dominion, because the whole of the edifice faced east. Outside the inner veil, but still inside the house, the table of the bread of the presence, the menorah, and the altar for incense were arranged. The house of God was just that: the place where he dwelled and where he might meet his people.

Immediately outside the house and down some steps, the altar itself, of unhewn stones and accessible by ramps and steps, was arranged. Priests tended to the sacrifices, and other male Israelites were also admitted into the court structure that surrounded the altar. Various specialized structures accommodated the needs of the priests, and chambers were built into the interior of the court (and, indeed, within the house) to serve as storerooms, treasuries, and the like. The bronze gate of Nicanor led eastward again, down steps to the court of the women, where female Israelites in a state of purity were admitted. Priests and Israelites might enter the complex of house and courts by means of gates along the north and south walls; priests and Levites who were actively engaged in the service of the sanctuary tended to use the north side.

The complex we have so far described, which is commonly known as the sanctuary proper, circumscribed the God, the people, and the offerings of Israel. Within the boundaries of the sanctuary, what was known to be pure was offered by personnel chosen for the purpose, in the presence of the people of God and of God himself. Nothing foreign, no one with a serious defect or impurity, and nothing unclean were permitted. Here God's presence was marked as much by order as by the pillar of cloud that was the flag of the Temple by day and the embers that glowed at night. God was present to the people with the things he had made and chosen for his own, and their presence brought them into the benefits of the covenantal compact with God. The practice of the Temple and its sacrificial worship were centered on the demarcation and the consumption of purity in its place, with the result that God's holiness could be safely enjoyed, within his four walls, and the walls of male and female Israel. In no other place on earth was Israel more Israel, or God more God, than in the sanctuary. A balustrade surrounded the sanctuary, and steps led down to the exterior court: non-Israelites who entered were threatened with death. Physically and socially, the sanctuary belonged to none but God and what and whom God chose, and then only in their places.

The sanctuary itself was enclosed by a larger court, and the edifice as a whole was referred to as the Temple. On the north side the pure sacrificial animals were slain and butchered, and stone pillars and tables, chains, rings and ropes, and vessels and bushels were arranged to enable the process to go on smoothly and with visible, deliberate rectitude. The north side of the sanctuary, then, was essentially devoted to the preparation of what could be offered, under the ministration of those who were charged with the offering itself. The south side was the most readily accessible area in the Temple. Although Israelites outnumbered any other group of people there and pious Jews entered only unshod, without staff or purse (cf. Mishnah *Berakhoth* 9:5), others might enter through the triple gate on the south wall of the mount of the Temple; the elaborate system of pools, cisterns, and conduits to the south of the mount, visible today, evidences the practice of ritual purity, no doubt by all entrants, whether Jewish or Gentile, into the Temple. Basically, then, the south side of the outer court was devoted to people, and the north side to things; together, the entire area of the outer court might be described as potentially chosen, while the sanctuary defined what actually had been chosen. The outer court was itself held in the highest regard, as is attested architecturally by the elaborate gates around the mount.

The Gospels describe the southern side of the outer court as the place where Jesus expelled the traders, and that is what brings us to the question of a dispute in which Pharisees were involved. The exterior court was unquestionably well suited for trade, since it was surrounded by porticos on the inside, in conformity with Herod's architectural preferences. But the assumption of Rabbinic literature and Josephus is that the market for the sale of sacrificial beasts was not located in the Temple at all but in a place called Ḥanuth (meaning "market" in Aramaic) on the Mount of Olives, across the Kidron Valley. According to the Babylonian Talmud (*'Abodah Zarah* 8b; *Shabbath* 15a; *Sanhedrin* 41a), some forty years before the destruction of the Temple the principal council of Jerusalem was removed from the place in the Temple called the Chamber of Hewn Stone to Ḥanuth. Around 30 CE, Caiaphas expelled the Sanhedrin and introduced the traders into the Temple, in both ways centralizing power in his own hands.

From the point of view of Pharisaism generally, trade in the southern side of the outer court was anathema. Purses were not permitted in the Temple according to the Pharisees' teaching, and the introduction of trade into the Temple rendered the ideal of not bringing into the Temple more than would be consumed there impracticable. Incidentally, the installation of traders in the porticos necessitated the removal of those teachers, Pharisaic and otherwise, who taught and observed in the Temple itself (see Babylonian Talmud *Sanhedrin* 11b; *Pesaḥim* 26a).

From the point of view of the smooth conduct of sacrifice, of course, Caiaphas's innovation was sensible. One could know at the moment of purchase that one's sacrifice was acceptable and not run the risk of harm befalling the animal on its way to be slaughtered. But when we look at the installation of the traders from the point of view of Hillel's teaching, Jesus' objection becomes understandable. Hillel had taught that one's sacrifice had to be shown to be one's own by the imposition of hands; part of the necessary preparation was not just of people to the south and beasts to the north but the connection between the two by appropriation. Caiaphas's innovation was sensible on the understanding that sacrifice was simply a matter of offering pure, unblemished animals. But it failed in Pharisaic terms, not only in its introduction of the necessity for commerce into the Temple, but in its breach of the link between worshiper and offering in the sacrificial action. The animals were correct in Caiaphas's system, and the priests regular, but the understanding of the offering as by the chosen people appeared — to some at least — profoundly defective.

The essential component of Jesus' occupation of the Temple is perfectly explicable within the context of contemporary Pharisaism, in which purity was more than a question of animals for sacrifice being intact. For Jesus, the issue of sacrifice also — and crucially — concerned the action of Israel, as in the teaching of Hillel. His action, of course, upset financial arrangements for the sale of such animals, and it is interesting that John 2:15 speaks of his sweeping away the "coins" (in Greek, *kermata*) involved in the trade. But such incidental disturbance is to be distinguished from a deliberate attempt to prevent the collection of the half shekel. That would have required coordinated activity throughout Israel and beyond and at issue would be much larger units of currency than the term "coins" would suggest.

Jesus shared Hillel's concern that what was offered by Israel in the Temple should truly belong to Israel. His vehemence in opposition to Caiaphas's reform was a function of his deep commitment to the notion that Israel was pure and should offer of its own, even if others thought one unclean (see Matt. 8:2-4; Mark 1:40-44; Luke 5:12-14), on the grounds that it is not what goes into a person that defiles, but what comes out of a person (see Matt. 15:11; Mark 7:15). Israelites are properly understood as pure, so that what extends from a person, what one is and does and has, manifests that purity. That focused, generative vision was the force behind Jesus' occupation of the Temple; only those after 70 CE who no longer treasured the Temple in Jerusalem as God's house could (mis)take Jesus' position to be an unqualified prophecy of doom or a global objection to sacrifice. When Jesus cited Jer. 7:11 in equating Caiaphas's arrangement in the Temple with theft, he implicitly invoked Jeremiah's prophecy of the Temple's destruction (see Matt. 21:13; Mark 11:17; Luke 19:46, discussed on pp. 91-94). But the implication was only that and was exaggerated by Caiaphas for one purpose and later by non-Judaic Christians for another purpose. The force of Jesus' message concerned what the Temple should be, not its demolition.

Jesus' Crucifixion and the Kingdom of God

Jesus' interference in the ordinary worship of the Temple might have been sufficient by itself to bring about his execution. After all, the Temple was the center of Judaism for as long as it stood. Roman officials were so interested in its smooth functioning at the hands of the priests they appointed that they were known to sanction the penalty of death for gross sacrilege.[27] Yet there is no indication that Jesus was arrested immediately. Instead, he remained at liberty for some time and was finally taken into custody just after one of his meals (Matt. 26:47-56; Mark 14:43-52; Luke 22:47-53; John 18:3-11). The decision of the authorities of the Temple to move against Jesus when they did is what made that meal the "last supper."

Why did the authorities wait, and why did they act when they did? The Gospels portray them as fearful of the popular backing that Jesus enjoyed (Matt. 26:5; Mark 14:2; Luke 22:2; John 11:47-48), and his inclusive teaching of purity probably did bring enthusiastic followers into the Temple with him. But there was another factor: Jesus could not simply be dispatched as a cultic criminal. He was not attempting an onslaught on the Temple as such; his dispute with the authorities concerned purity within the Temple. Other rabbis of his period also engaged in physical demonstrations of the purity they required in the conduct of worship, as we have seen (pp. 118-119 above). Jesus' action was extreme, but not totally without precedent, even in the use of force. Most crucially, Jesus could claim the support of tradition in objecting to placing vendors in the Temple, and Caiaphas's innovation in fact did not stand, so that the Rabbinic sources could later assume that Ḥanuth was where the vendors were normally located.

The delay of the authorities, then, was understandable. We could also say it was commendable, reflecting continued controversy over the merits of Jesus' teaching and whether his occupation of the great court should be condemned out of hand. But why did they finally arrest Jesus? The last supper provides the key; something about Jesus' meals after his occupation of the Temple caused Judas to inform on Jesus. Of course, "Judas" is the only name that the traditions of the New Testament have left us. We cannot say who or how many of the disciples became disaffected by Jesus' behavior after his occupation of the Temple.

However they learned of Jesus' new interpretation of his meals of fellowship, the authorities arrested him just after the supper we call last. Jesus continued to celebrate fellowship at table as a foretaste of the kingdom, just as he had before. As before, the promise of drinking wine new in the kingdom of God joined his followers in an anticipatory celebration of the kingdom (see Matt. 26:29; Mark 14:25; Luke 22:18, discussed in the last chapter, pp. 85-90). But he also added a new and

27. See Josephus, *Antiquities* 15.417.

scandalous dimension of meaning. His occupation of the Temple having failed, Jesus said over the wine "This is my blood," and over the bread "This is my flesh" (Matt. 26:26, 28; Mark 14:22, 24; Luke 22:19-20; 1 Cor. 11:24-25; Justin, *Apology* I.66.3).

In Jesus' context, the context of his confrontation with the authorities of the Temple, his words can have had only one meaning. He cannot have meant "Here are my personal body and blood"; that is an interpretation that only makes sense at a later stage in the development of Christianity.[28] Jesus' point was rather that, in the absence of a Temple that permitted his view of purity to be practiced, wine was his blood of sacrifice and bread was his flesh of sacrifice. In Aramaic, "blood" *(dᵉma)* and "flesh" *(bisra,* which may also be rendered as "body") can carry such a sacrificial meaning, and in Jesus' context, that is the most natural meaning.

The meaning of "the last supper," then, actually evolved over a series of meals after Jesus' occupation of the Temple. During that period, Jesus claimed that wine and bread were a better sacrifice than what was offered in the Temple, a foretaste of the new wine in the kingdom of God. At least wine and bread were Israel's own, not tokens of priestly dominance. No wonder the opposition to him, even among the Twelve (in the shape of Judas, according to the Gospels), became deadly. In essence, Jesus made his meals into a rival altar.

That final gesture of protest gave Caiaphas what he needed. Jesus could be charged with blasphemy before those with an interest in the Temple. The issue now was not simply Jesus' opposition to where animals for sacrifice were sold, but his creation of an alternative *cultus.* He blasphemed the law of Moses.[29] The accusation concerned the Temple, in which Rome also had a vested interest. Pilate had no regard for issues of purity; Acts 18:14-16 reflects the attitude of an official in a similar position, and Josephus shows that Pilate was without sympathy for

---

28. For a discussion of that development as reflected within the texts of the New Testament, see *A Feast of Meanings.* In a general way, the question is also treated in B. Chilton, "The Eucharist: Exploring Its Origins," *Bible Review* 10.6 (1994) 36-43.

29. Such an interpretation obviates defining the "blasphemy" as either formal, as in Mishnah *Sanhedrin* 7:5, or as a matter of christology (cf. Rudolf Pesch, *Das Markusevangelium* II [Herders Theologischer Kommentar zum Neuen Testament; Freiburg: Herder, 1980] 440). Josephus can refer to attacks on Jews (*Apion* 1.59, 223), on Moses (*Antiquities* 3.307; *Apion* 1.279), or on patriarchal law (*Apion* 2.143) as blasphemy (cf. Herman Wolfgang Beyer, "βλασφημέω . . .," *Theological Dictionary of the New Testament* I, ed. G. Kittel, tr. G. W. Bromiley [Grand Rapids: Eerdmans, 1978] 621-625).

Judaism.[30] But the Temple in Jerusalem had come to symbolize Roman power as well as the devotion of Israel. Rome guarded jealously the sacrifices that the emperor financed in Jerusalem; when they were spurned in the year 66, the act was a declaration of war (see Josephus, *War* 2.409). Jesus stood accused of creating a disturbance in that Temple (during his occupation) and of fomenting disloyalty to it and (therefore) to Caesar. Pilate did what he had to do. Jesus' persistent reference to a "kingdom" that Caesar did not rule and his repute among some as messiah or prophet only made Pilate's order more likely. It all was probably done without a hearing; Jesus was not a Roman citizen. He was a nuisance, dispensed with under a military jurisdiction.[31]

At last, then, at the end of his life, Jesus discovered the public center of the kingdom: the point from which the light of God's rule would radiate and triumph. His initial intention was that the Temple would conform to his vision of the purity of the kingdom, that all Israel would be invited there, forgiven and forgiving, to offer of their own in divine fellowship in the confidence that what they produced was pure (see Matt. 15:11; Mark 7:15, discussed in the last chapter, pp. 81-82). The innovation of Caiaphas prevented that, by erecting what Jesus (as well as other rabbis) saw as an unacceptable barrier between Israel and what Israel offered.

The last public act of Jesus before his crucifixion was to declare that his meals were the center of the kingdom. What was near and immanent and final and pure was now understood to radiate from a public place, an open manifestation of God's rule. The authorities in the Temple had rejected what some people in Galilee already had. Just as those in the north could be condemned as a new Sodom (see Luke 10:12), so Jesus could deny that offerings coopted by priests were acceptable sacrifices. It is no coincidence that the typical setting of appearances of the risen Jesus is while disciples were taking meals together.[32] The conviction that the light of the kingdom radiated from that practice went hand in hand with the conviction that the true master of the table, the rabbi who began it all, remained with their fellowship.

---

30. Pilate's outrages are described on the basis of Philo and Josephus in F. F. Bruce, *New Testament History* (London: Pickering and Inglis, 1969/Garden City: Doubleday, 1971) 32-36.

31. See Paul Winter, *On the Trial of Jesus* (Studia Judaica; Berlin: de Gruyter, 1961) 62-66.

32. Luke 24:13-35, 36-43; Mark 16:14-18 (not originally part of the Gospel, but an early witness of the resurrection nonetheless); John 21:1-14.

CHAPTER 6

Copying the Copy

Jesus' Preaching within Primitive Christianity

Jesus' conception of the kingdom, conveyed by word and action, represented as clear a vision of divine activity as his contemporaries could have wished. God was held to be initiating his final intervention in human affairs. In so doing, God was displacing evil with his kingdom, demanding righteousness, creating purity, and providing a center, a public representation of that kingdom.

Only Jesus' dramatic confrontation with the authorities of the Temple at the end of his life fully defined that last dimension of the kingdom, the point from which and the horizon toward which the kingdom was radiating. Whatever may have been the case at the beginning of his ministry, by the end Jesus' contemporaries were not puzzled by what he said about the kingdom. His teaching and his deeds were both copies of his vision of God's activity, parables in words and gestures that made his vision explicit. One could agree or disagree or ignore what Jesus said and did, but to claim not to understand his message would have been disingenuous. The gospel of Jesus[1] was crafted too carefully in the language of early Judaism to be dismissed as irrelevant symbolism.

---

1. "Gospel" here is used in the Aramaic sense *(besora')*: it refers to the triumphant news of God's victory, as in the Targum of Isaiah 53:1. For the linkage of that usage to Jesus' usage, see B. Chilton, *God in Strength: Jesus' Announcement of the Kingdom* (Studien zum Neuen Testament und seiner Umwelt 1; Freistadt: Plöchl, 1979), reprinted in the Biblical Seminar series (Sheffield: JSOT, 1987) 93-95.

Parabolic speech and action were necessary within Jesus' ministry, because his task was to re-present, to copy. The kingdom that he perceived and participated in came to expression through his teaching (see chapter 4) and through the program of active discipleship (see chapter 5) that he promulgated. His copy could only be understood by being copied, being re-presented anew in the apprehension and action and teaching of those who followed him.[2]

This is not the moment to analyze the resurrection in any detail; that is a topic with its own history of generation within primitive Christianity. But we can observe that the fact that Jesus was thought to have taught about the kingdom after his death (see Acts 1:3) was fundamental to the continuation of the movement he began. The conviction of his personal presence with his followers during their meals of the kingdom (discussed on pp. 123-126 above) was the warrant that his teaching of the kingdom had been true. Just as Moses and Elijah were witnesses of the kingdom of God (see Matt. 16:28; Mark 9:1; Luke 9:27, discussed on pp. 62-65), so now Jesus stood as the primary testator of the kingdom. Divine activity and Jesus' presence were experienced together. That is a defining characteristic of primitive Christianity, the continuation of Jesus' movement within early Judaism after the resurrection.[3]

The Catechesis of the Kingdom

The movement of Jesus may be regarded as having started from the moment his preaching of the kingdom was accepted. Accepting his theme that the kingdom was dawning naturally involved a desire to

---

2. See Marianne Sawicki, *Seeing the Lord: Resurrection and Early Christian Practices* (Minneapolis: Fortress, 1994). Her last chapter, "Copy Who Copies" (pp. 301-336), includes a good discussion of the hermeneutics of copying, as commonly understood in post-modern discussion. My own perspective is developed in *The Temple of Jesus: His Sacrificial Program within a Cultural History of Sacrifice* (University Park: Pennsylvania State University, 1992), Appendix 1: "A Response to *Things Hidden from the Foundation of the World*," 163-172.

3. The term "early Christianity" should be reserved for the emergence of the movement as a replacement of Judaism. That emergence occurred with the Epistle to the Hebrews. For discussion, see B. Chilton and Jacob Neusner, *Judaism in the New Testament: Practices and Beliefs* (London: Routledge, 1995).

enjoy the kingdom's light. How could one be among the many who were to feast in the kingdom, and not among those who were to be excluded? Jesus' own response to such issues within the movement is largely contained in the instruction for his disciples known as Q, as we have seen in chapter 5. In respect of social function, Jesus' instruction of his closest followers is to be distinguished from the catechetical program for beginners, of which the Synoptic Gospels are examples, but the agenda of preparing adherents of the movement is shared by Q and the Synoptics. In both cases, as well, the conviction of Jesus' resurrection is a pivotal factor in the presentation of Jesus' teaching and status.

The Kingdom in Q

A characteristic feature of Q is to present its earliest stage, the mishnah of Jesus, in a way that makes it possible to understand his own preaching (as we have seen in chapter 4). The compilation of that mishnah in Aramaic ca. 35 CE occurred in circumstances that were generally favorable to the preservation of Jesus' message in an oral environment. In the year 36, Caiaphas himself was removed from office (together with Pilate, his protector) by the Syrian legate Vitellius (so Josephus, *Antiquities* 18.90-95).[4] His innovation of installing vendors in the Temple can not have survived his removal, so the disciples of Jesus had access to a better-regulated Temple than Jesus did (from their point of view), and there is no reason to suppose they could not have circulated freely in Judaea and Galilee, as Q insists they should.

But the composition of Q in its Syrian phase, a decade later, presupposes a significant rejection of the message of Jesus.[5] The eschatological woes pronounced against Chorazin, Bethsaida, and Capernaum (Luke 10:13-15), for example, reflect refusal of Jesus' emissaries.[6]

---

4. At the same time, Vitellius released the high-priestly vestments from custody in the Roman fortress adjacent to the Temple known as the Antonia. For further discussion, see *The Temple of Jesus,* 107-109.

5. The development of Q has already been discussed in chapter 5 (pp. 107-110). In each case, the citation of Luke here presupposes that the Matthean form of the material is also in view.

6. See the discussion in David Catchpole, *The Quest for Q* (Edinburgh: Clark, 1993) 171-176; Leif E. Vaage, *Galilean Upstarts: Jesus' First Followers According to Q* (Valley Forge: Trinity Press International, 1994) 108, 117.

During Jesus' own ministry, Capernaum had provided a model of success (see Luke 4:23); its later resistance — along with more prominent places such as Bethsaida — provoked a bitter reaction. Deprived of the hospitality that would have been a mark of the acceptance of their message, the community of Q wore its poverty as a badge of honor. Out of this situation arose the virtual equation of poverty and the kingdom that is such a strong feature of several sayings, especially the first beatitude: "Blessed are the poor, because the kingdom of God is yours" (Luke 6:20).

The blessing of the poor is linked to a scenario in which the rich are to suffer. Moreover, the poor are associated with those who are abused "for the sake of the son of man" and the rich with those who embraced the false prophets of old (Luke 6:20-26). The social situation could hardly be plainer, as David Catchpole has observed:

> Here, then, by employing the language of opposition which, however, falls short of separation, and by building on earlier use of the deuteronomic pattern of perpetually persecuted prophets, which had been employed (as it were) domestically within Israel, the editor allows us a glimpse of a situation within the community of Israel.[7]

Tension is rising in Israel as a result of the attempt after the resurrection to implement Jesus' charge to his disciples. Jesus is now understood as "the son of man," a phrase that in Catchpole's words "conveys the heavenly status and future coming in judgment of the Jesus who had been known on earth." That keen sense of what the future is to bring, the reversal in standing of oppressor and oppressed, developed into the apocalyptic assurance that also characterizes Q. The people of Q know they are the "little flock" to whom the kingdom has been given; only a brief interval separates them from their reward (Luke 12:32). The judgment of the kingdom is to be as severe as Q's parable of the returning king (Luke 19:11-27).[8]

---

7. Catchpole, *The Quest for Q*, 94. The entire discussion, pp. 81-94, should be required reading for those who assume that any reference to poverty can only have come from Jesus; see Vaage, *Galilean Upstarts*, 56-57, 107.

8. Of course, there may be dominical elements in the sayings mentioned here (see, for example, Luke 12:31; Matt. 6:33). But in their present form, they tell us more about the community of Q than about Jesus.

The Kingdom in the Petrine Cycle

The self-consciousness of the movement around Jesus as a group apart from other sorts of Judaism, a self-consciousness that emerges after the resurrection, is articulated clearly in the Petrine circle of tradition. As we have seen in chapter 4 (pp. 62-65), the circle of Peter framed its catechesis around 35 CE and preserved what are evidently sayings of Jesus himself. The assurance of the kingdom in the name of those who do not taste death (Matt. 16:28; Mark 9:1; Luke 9:27) and Jesus' saying regarding wealth and the kingdom of God (Matt. 19:24; Mark 10:25; Luke 18:25; see pp. 76-77 above) stand out as prominent examples. But the Petrine cycle did not simply transmit such sayings.

The promise concerning those who will never taste death is followed immediately by the Transfiguration (Matt. 17:1-9; Mark 9:2-10; Luke 9:28-36). Peter, James, and John are taken up a mountain by Jesus, whose own appearance changes prior to the arrival of Moses and Elijah. The three privileged disciples, Peter at their head, are there to see the promise of the kingdom in terms reminiscent of Moses' ascent of Sinai with three privileged followers (Exod. 24:1-11). Here are the emblems of the Petrine catechesis: Jesus is related to God as Moses once was, and Peter is his Aaron, a witness that the kingdom has been covenanted.

The Transfiguration is a good example of the Petrine cycle generally. Part of that cycle's program is to portray Peter, James, and John as the best representatives of Jesus. They are the most prominent among the first of the disciples called (Mark 1:16-20),[9] the only disciples present at the raising of Jairus's daughter (Mark 5:21-24, 35-43) as well as at the Transfiguration, and Jesus' companions in Gethsemane (Mark 14:32-42). When Paul visited Peter in Jerusalem, he stayed with Peter fifteen days (Gal. 1:18) and knew him as "Cephas," the Aramaic nickname (for "rock") that Jesus had given him. Paul insists that he saw only Cephas and James, the brother of Jesus (Gal. 1:19-20). The Petrine cycle as it appears in Mark is the closest approximation available of the catechesis that Peter used with Paul and other converts, and Paul's reference establishes that the Petrine cycle existed by the year 35.[10]

---

9. As Q is cited according to its appearance in Luke, so the Petrine cycle should be cited according to its appearance in Mark.

10. On the issue of chronology, see Jürgen Becker, *Paul: Apostle to the Gentiles,* tr. O. C. Dean (Louisville: Westminster/John Knox, 1993) 17-32.

The Transfiguration appears in tight association with Jesus' assurance concerning those who will never taste death. The effect of that association is to warrant Peter, James, and John as the best interpreters of Jesus' teaching. That comes as no surprise, because Jesus' teaching is held to hinge on the issue of discipleship: who better to explain it than the first and most intimate of Jesus' disciples? The assurance of the kingdom in Mark 9:1 is preceded by the promise that everyone who denies himself, takes up his cross, and follows Jesus — even to the point of losing his life — will save his life (Mark 8:34-39). So presented, the saying regarding those "standing here" would seem to be a promise of life for loyal disciples until the *eschaton*. That was the meaning imputed to the saying in the Petrine cycle, in which Peter represents the exalted status of discipleship.

The disciples' exaltation comes at a price in the Petrine cycle. They need to lose their lives before they are saved. By the same logic, they need to give up what Peter calls "everything" in the way of possessions for the kingdom (Mark 10:28). Jesus elaborates the point: house, family, and field have to be offered up for the kingdom in order for the greater house, family, and field to be possessed (vv. 29-30). That is the meaning, within the Petrine circle, of the saying about the camel and the rich man, a meaning that could only be realized in the practice of the Petrine circle. There, commonality of goods was as characteristic as eucharist and worship in the Temple (see Acts 2:42-47; 5:1-11).

Practical discipleship as a discipline of learning what to give up for the Lord Jesus is a paramount concern in the Petrine cycle. That is why even Peter and his companions are made to look silly until that lesson is learned (see, for example, Mark 9:6 and 14:37-38, 40). The power of discipleship lies not simply in being called by Jesus and becoming intimate with him. It requires that one learns what Jesus exemplified, that life be lost in order to be regained. That is the way into the kingdom.

The Kingdom in James's Interpretation

Paul refers to James only in passing in Gal. 1:19, but James was Paul's nemesis at Antioch, as Paul attests in Gal. 2:11-21. Paul claims that when Cephas was in Antioch Cephas was accustomed to eat with Gentiles, but then when representatives of James arrived, Cephas deferred to them and separated himself from his former association (2:12). Indeed, Paul has to admit that even Barnabas was convinced to follow the Jacobean policy (v. 13). By this time, then, James was the single most influential leader in the primitive Church, and his authority reached far beyond his own circle.

When Acts gives an account of the Jacobean policy toward Gentiles, James appears much more sympathetic than he does in Galatians. But his rigor cannot be mistaken. The occasion of his statement of policy is said to be the suggestion that men must be circumcised in order to be saved (Acts 15:1), a suggestion associated with a form of Christian Pharisaism (15:5). Peter is said to side with Paul, insisting that Jews and Gentiles be treated alike since God gives his spirit to both (see 15:7-11). James agrees that Gentiles who turn to God are not to be encumbered (v. 19), and yet he insists that they be instructed by letter to abstain "from the pollutions of idols, from fornication, from what is strangled, and from blood" (v. 20). In effect, he reverses the policy of not making a distinction between Jews and Gentiles by requiring Gentiles to adhere to basic rules of purity.

The grounds given for the Jacobean policy are that the law of Moses is commonly acknowledged (Acts 15:21); the implication is that to disregard such elemental considerations of purity as James specifies would be to dishonor Moses. Judas Barsabbas and Silas are then dispatched with Paul and Barnabas to deliver the letter in Antioch along with their personal testimony (vv. 22-29), and are said particularly to continue their instruction as prophets (vv. 32, 33). They refer to the regulations of purity as necessities (v. 28), and no amount of Lukan gloss can conceal that what they insist on is a serious reversal of Paul's position (see 1 Corinthians 8). The dispatch of Judas and Silas implicitly undermines the standing of Paul and Barnabas, and James's policy amounts to a constraint upon the behavior of Gentiles who joined the movement.[11] Because the meeting concerning Gentiles in the Church occurred in 49 CE, we can say that by that time the Jacobean catechesis existed in Greek (for communication in Antioch). In an Aramaic form, it was probably composed ca. 40 CE.[12]

11. The constraints are sometimes compared to the so-called Noachic commandments of Babylonian Talmud *Sanhedrin* 56b; see Kirsopp Lake, "The Apostolic Council of Jerusalem," in *The Acts of the Apostles* V, ed. F. J. Foakes Jackson and K. Lake (reprint, Grand Rapids: Baker, 1979) 195-212, 208.

12. After all, Paul seems not to have been made aware of it during his visit in 35 CE. The Jacobean source was less an independent cycle than a recasting of the Petrine cycle. Its contents included Mark 4:3-20; 7:6-13; 14:12-16.

The signature of the Jacobean circle is detectable in Matt. 13:10-11; Mark 4:10-11; Luke 8:9-10, where it is claimed that Jesus conveys the secret(s) of the kingdom to the larger group of twelve disciples, the precursor of what has come to be called the apostolic college in Jerusalem.[13] The group concerned is not the select company around Peter, but those of Jesus' disciples who devote themselves to the authoritative interpretation of his teaching. Indeed, the passage occurs immediately prior to Jesus' explanation of the parable of the sower, which is the foundation of the collection of parables in all three Synoptics. The message of the Jacobean group is that the company of James enjoys particular insight into the kingdom and that the kingdom is essentially a didactic matter, into which Jesus' disciples offer initiation.

The Kingdom in the Synoptic Gospels

With little formal change, then, but with mastery of the context of presentation, the circles of Q, of Peter, and of James were able to control and transform the meaning of the kingdom. In each, a principle of privilege was claimed for the particular circle involved and its traditional cycle. But at the same time, the meaning of the kingdom shifted in each case. What for Jesus was a divine intervention in the world (of time, space, action, objects, and humanity) became for the community of Q a blessing in the form of future reward, for the Petrine group the assurance of the power of faithful discipleship, and for the Jacobean group a method of authoritative interpretation (for example, in the explanation of parables).

Transformation by means of context is also evident in the other circles that fed the Synoptic Gospels, although the impact of their changes appears less dramatic. Reference has repeatedly been made here to Jesus' promise of the inclusion of many from east and west in the patriarchal feast of the kingdom (Matt. 8:11-12; Luke 13:28-29; see pp. 81-82 above). The mishnaic source in which that saying was included was marked by a tendency to be directed against the Jewish opponents of the movement. In the Matthean version, the saying appears as an addendum to the healing of the servant of the Roman centurion and

13. B. Chilton, *A Galilean Rabbi and His Bible: Jesus' Use of the Interpreted Scripture of His Time* (Wilmington: Glazier, 1984), also published with the subtitle *Jesus' Own Interpretation of Isaiah* (London: SPCK, 1984) 90-97.

with an explicit warning against "the sons of the kingdom" (v. 12). In the Lukan version, the saying is presented as part of a discourse concerning salvation, in which hearers are warned that merely having enjoyed Jesus' company during his lifetime is no guarantee of fellowship with the patriarchs in the eschatological feast (13:22-30). The differences between the two versions make the supposition of a fixed, written "Q" appear implausible at this point, and they commend the model of an instructional source that was susceptible of local variation.

Even at a later stage, context could result in variegated portrayals of the kingdom. Before we discuss what is achieved by contextualization in each Synoptic Gospel, however, it is necessary to explain that there is a commonly Synoptic transformation of the kingdom, a transformation that is plausibly associated with the circle of Barnabas in Antioch. The transformation is sufficiently general that each Synoptic Gospel's construal may be described as a variation on a theme, while it is so distinctive that no other ancient document may be described as sharing it. The transformation introduces the kingdom as preached by Jesus.[14] This obvious feature of the Gospels' narratives is no less influential for being evident: the kingdom from this point on is established as the burden of Jesus' message and no other's. Moreover, acceptance of him involves embracing the characteristic understanding of the kingdom that unfolds. Mark 1:15 is the best representative of the Barnaban summary of Jesus' preaching, and in fact it is a fair representation.

The next major phase in the Synoptic transformation of the kingdom is pedagogical. The Jesus who is the kingdom's herald is also its advocate, the one who explains its features to those who hear and yet are puzzled (or even scandalized). The extent of the material each Gospel devotes to this phase varies greatly, but in every case it is the largest phase.[15] The distribution of this material also varies, but it is striking that none of the Synoptic Gospels invokes the term "kingdom" as a link to include all statements on the subject in a single complex of material. Such an association by catchword is indeed detectable over

---

14. Matt. 4:17, 23; 9:35; 12:28; Mark 1:15; Luke 4:43; 8:1; 9:2; 10:9, 11; 11:20.

15. Matt. 5:3, 10, 19, 20; 6:10, 33; 7:21; 8:11, 12; 11:12; 13:11, 19, 24, 31, 33, 38, 41, 43, 44, 45, 47, 52; 16:19; 18:1, 3, 4, 23; 19:12, 14, 23; 20:1; 21:31, 43; 22:2; 23:14; 24:14; 25:1, 34; Mark 4:11, 26, 30; 9:1, 47; 10:14, 15, 23, 24, 25; 12:34; Luke 6:20; 7:28; 8:1, 10; 9:11, 27, 60, 62; 11:2; 12:31; 13:18, 20, 28, 29; 16:16; 17:20, 21; 18:16, 17, 24, 25, 29; 21:31.

short runs of material, so that isolated sayings are the exception, not the rule; but in no case is subject matter or wording the sole determinative influence on context. Rather, there is a narrative contextualization in which Jesus' activity in preaching, teaching, and disputing becomes the governing framework for a given run of sayings. Those frameworks vary from Gospel to Gospel, of course, as do the sayings presented; the distribution of sayings can certainly not be explained by reference to some fixed, historical ordering. The point is rather that the typically Synoptic transformation of Jesus' preaching embeds the kingdom within his ministry, so that he and the kingdom approximate interchangeability. The particular textual moves that achieve this identification vary, but that it is achieved does not.

The last phase of the Synoptic transformation of the kingdom pursues the logic of the identification: Jesus' death and the kingdom are presented as mutually explicating. "I will not drink of the fruit of the vine again until I drink it with you new in God's kingdom" (cf. Matt. 26:29; Mark 14:25; Luke 22:18). Whatever the sense of that saying was within the ministry of Jesus (see pp. 85-90 above), within the Synoptics it serves to insist that the same Jesus who announced and taught the kingdom is also the sole guarantor of its glorious coming.

The Synoptic transformation of the kingdom essentially involves a unique pattern of distribution of sayings and of their narrative contextualization within Jesus' ministry. The result is to focus on Jesus as the herald, advocate, and guarantor of the kingdom in an innovative fashion. Arguably, the transformation makes explicit what is implicit in the sayings tradition: an awareness that Jesus' ministry is a seal of the kingdom. The most obvious instance of such a claim in his sayings is Jesus' observation concerning his exorcisms and the kingdom (Matt. 12:28; Luke 11:20; see pp. 67-70 above). But such implications are no more than that, and observing them only heightens by contrast the Synoptic transformation, in which Jesus' preaching of the kingdom becomes the seal of his divine mission, not the principal point at issue. He who witnessed the kingdom is, in the Synoptics, attested as God's son by virtue of his own message. Precisely because a signal adjustment of precedence between Jesus and the kingdom has taken place, the language of "transformation" is appropriate.

In view of its distinctiveness from the sense of the kingdom in other documents of early Judaism and Christianity, the Synoptic transformation is a particular framing of Jesus' sayings, not merely a loose characterization of similar material in three Gospels. How the transformation was effected, whether by literary borrowing from one document to another or by sharing of a now lost antecedent, is a matter of conjecture.[16]

Although each of the Synoptic Gospels substantially conveys the Barnaban transformation of the kingdom, each construes it distinctively. That is perhaps most easily appreciated by considering how Jesus' initial preaching is presented. In Matthew, Jesus says "Repent, for the kingdom of heaven is at hand" (4:17), but he is not the first to do so. John is portrayed as delivering the same message (3:2). Part of the authority of the Matthean Jesus is that he is the climax of the prophetic witness that went before him; in Matthew alone, Jesus consciously decides to preach in Galilee, and his decision is held to fulfill a passage from the book of Isaiah (4:12-16). Mark has no such reference, but it does uniquely have Jesus say, "Repent, *and believe in the gospel*" (1:15c). That is an effective way to link Jesus' preaching to the preaching about him, and Mark's Gospel alone begins with "The beginning of the gospel . . ." (1:1). As if to underline the point, Jesus' announcement of the kingdom is itself called "the gospel of God" (1:14). The most confident equation between the kingdom and the one who preaches it is offered in Luke. Although it is assumed that Jesus preaches the kingdom (4:43), the instance of initial preaching that precedes that notice has Jesus quoting Scripture to the effect that he is God's anointed (4:16-21).

The narrative identification of the progress of the kingdom with Jesus' own ministry is of the essence of the transformation of traditions that generated the Synoptic Gospels. Part of that transformation is the unequivocal belief that Jesus is to be the agent, along with God, in the final judgment of the kingdom. Much as the book of Isaiah provided the principal image of the festivity of the kingdom, the book of Daniel provided the principal image of Jesus' role in that judgment. In Daniel, four beasts represent the great empires that were to rule from Daniel's time (Babylon, Persia, Media, and Greece). After the beasts are described, God appears on his throne (7:9-10); "one like a son of man," a human being, is presented to God and receives total dominion (7:13-14). In Daniel itself,

---

16. The history of such speculation is impressively given objective standing by referring to it as "the Synoptic Problem," as if it were a phenomenon of texts rather than a disturbance among interpreters. Cf. Chilton, *Profiles of a Rabbi: Synoptic Opportunities in Reading about Jesus* (Brown Judaic Studies 177; Atlanta: Scholars Press, 1989).

the figure is essentially an agent of redemption and disclosure within the heavenly court. The faith of early Christians identified Jesus with that angelic vision.[17] At the moment when Jesus is interrogated by the authorities of the Temple, in the absence of any witness from the company of disciples, he replies without equivocation to the question whether he is the messiah, by citing Daniel 7 (see Matt. 26:63-64; Mark 14:61-62; Luke 22:66-69). Jesus, as that son of man of whom Daniel spoke, was not merely an angelic figure, but was to return to earth to claim and vindicate his own. A complex of material in the Synoptics develops an apocalyptic scenario in which the most important elements are the destruction of the Temple and Jesus' coming as the triumphant son of man of Daniel 7 (see Matthew 24–25; Mark 13; Luke 21:5-36). The Synoptic identification of Jesus with the kingdom is therefore an accurate reflection of the eschatological expectation of early Christians. Among the Synoptic Gospels, however, only Matthew presents the kingdom in an apocalyptic manner, as part of the scenario of the end time.[18]

Reflection, Controversy, and Synthesis

Even our brief consideration of the catechetical stage reveals its formative influence on the meaning of the kingdom within the New Testament. Transformations of the meaning of the kingdom at that stage — particularly in the Barnaban phase, when the kingdom was integrated biographically with the preaching concerning Jesus — permitted the next developments to take place. Unless those catechetical transformations of the meaning of the kingdom are appreciated, the paradox of the apparent disappearance of the kingdom as an emphasis within early Christianity will remain.

The Gospel according to John effects a radical reduction in focus

17. See B. Chilton, "The Son of Man: Human and Heavenly," in *The Four Gospels 1992: Festschrift Frans Neirynck,* ed. F. van Segbroeck, C. M. Tuckett, G. van Belle, and J. Verheyden (BETL 100; Leuven, 1992) 203-218.

18. Sometimes Matthew presents new material (see 13:24-30, 36-43, 47-50; 16:19; 20:1-16; 21:13; 25:1-13, 31-46), which seems to represent a development of the tradition of discourse in Syria. This explains the analogy of Matt. 13:47-50 in *Thomas* 8. On other occasions Matthew simply repeats the reference to the kingdom from elsewhere in the material presented (so 5:10; 13:19).

on the kingdom: only one statement, about seeing (3:3) or entering (3:5) the kingdom, is ever made. Such explanation as is offered explicates the requirement for this experience: being born "from above" *(anōthen)* or "from water and spirit."[19] The assumption is that no explanation of the kingdom itself is required. The passage is rather designed to insist that baptism in Jesus' name — birth from above by water and spirit — alone permits of participation in the kingdom.

The distinctively Johannine fashioning of traditions concerning Jesus does not center on the kingdom, and that is a mark of its singularity. The focus now is on receiving Jesus in such a manner that one might become a child of God (1:12): the Gospel is so consumed with the discursive and narrative issue of attaining eternal life (cf. 3:16) that the kingdom, the vision of what is actually achieved at the point where the eternal meets the temporal, is taken as a matter of course. The issue for John is means, not ends, because the fourth Gospel is composed for those whose baptism — and whose previous, catechetical introduction to the kingdom — is taken for granted.

Paul also communicates with those who have already been catechized, but he is notoriously less trusting of how his readers have been introduced to the faith and of how they conceive of it. His frequently controversial purposes comport well with his manner of reference to the kingdom, which is typically by way of correction. His insistence that the kingdom of God is not to be confused with food and drink (Rom. 14:17) is not the truism it may at first appear to be. Paul makes his statement in the midst of an argument against both maintaining regulations of purity in diet *and* blatantly flouting customs of purity (14:13-23). Writing to the congregation in Rome near the end of his life (ca. 57 CE), Paul makes his assertion that the kingdom is available as "righteousness, peace, and joy in the holy spirit" to humanity as a whole (14:17), whatever their views of purity. The primitive association of the kingdom and eucharist, rooted in the practice of Jesus, here becomes the point of departure for insistence on the inclusive reach of the kingdom. That theme is of such importance, Paul claims, that it would be better not to eat at all than to risk contravening it (14:21).

Because the kingdom for Paul is effective for those who attain to the promises of God through baptism into Christ, he views it as what

---

19. *Anōthen* might be taken as "again," but that is how Nicodemus is presented in v. 4 as understanding the term, and he is a paradigm of how to misconstrue Jesus' teaching.

those who follow Christian ethics may "inherit." Even within the idiom of inheritance, however, Paul's formulation is typically negative: lists of those who will not inherit the kingdom of God (so in Gal. 5:19-21, ca. 53 CE; 1 Cor. 6:9, 10, ca. 56 CE). The foundational metaphor of inheritance is not an obvious development from earlier usage.[20]

Why should the kingdom now be inherited, rather than entered? The transformation obviously has implications for eschatology in that Paul's construction of the kingdom is more consistently future than Jesus'. He ridicules those in Corinth who fancy themselves already regnant (1 Cor. 4:8) and explicitly portrays the kingdom as beyond the inheritance of flesh and blood (15:50). But that moment of inheritance may be attained to, according to Paul, because Jesus — as life-giving spirit (15:45) — has prepared a spiritual people, fit for the resurrection of the dead (15:42-58). Paul's metaphor of inheritance agrees with his theology of spiritual transformation.

By the reflective and controversial stages of John and Paul, then, the increasing focus of interest is preparation for the kingdom by means of baptism into Christ and the ethical performance of the baptismal spirit. There are evident differences in regard to the temporal emphasis of eschatology. The ultimacy of the kingdom may be expressed as "above" any concern for time or sequence (as in John 3:3, 5), or as keyed to that future moment when (as Paul puts it) Christ hands over the kingdom to God (1 Cor. 15:24). In either case, the issue of systemic importance is that Christ effects the transfer of the believer (at baptism, and thereafter) from his or her previous condition into the realm of God.

The stages of catechesis, reflection, and controversy added nothing, for all the variations of emphasis they involved, to the dimensions implicit in Jesus' gospel of the kingdom. At the end of a generation of development, the kingdom remained God's realm: ultimate, transcendent, perfect, holy, inclusive. But he who had at first preached the kingdom was now at the forefront, explicitly and without compromise, as the means — and the only means — of access to the kingdom.

The stark character of that development is measurable by the phrase "kingdom of Christ," used interchangeably with "kingdom of God." The earliest usage appears in Col. 1:13, a letter attributed to Paul but emanating

---

20. It is rooted in a pattern of usage exemplified by Luke 12:32, where the kingdom is presented as an apocalyptic reward (cf. *God in Strength*, 231-250), a thought typical of the theology of Q, as we have seen above (pp. 129-130; see also Matt. 19:28; Luke 22:28-30).

from the circle of Timothy ca. A.D. 90. The putative authors — Paul and Timothy together (1:1, 2) — give thanks to the father for making believers worthy "of a share of the portion of saints in the light, who delivered us from the authority of the dark and transferred us into the kingdom of the son of his love . . ." (1:12, 13). The continuity with Pauline emphases is obvious here, as is the statement from approximately five years later in Eph. 5:5, where the putative Paul speaks of those who do not have "an inheritance in the kingdom of Christ and of God."[21]

The latest documents of the New Testament in the present case simply identify a systemic principle that had been active since at least the period of catechesis. Because baptism into Christ, prayer in the manner of Christ, ethical imitation of Christ, and eucharist in remembrance of Christ were the means of access to God's kingdom, functionally God's reign was also Christ's. All that could be said, then, of the kingdom of God in all its dimensions could also be said of what believers enjoyed as a result of their identification with Christ.

Conclusion

How shall we compare the kingdom of God? As in the parable of the mustard seed, which that question prefaces (Mark 4:30-32), the fundamental comparison must be to an activity, the royal force of God's rule. The activity of God is as purposeful as human activity and is possessed of the same dimensions: time, effects, character, preferred objects and persons, and typical place (see chapter 4 above). Primitive Christianity inherited those coordinates from early Judaism because the evolution of primitive Christian theology presupposed Jesus' conception of the kingdom and remained fiercely loyal to it.

In early Judaism, God's royal activity was variously understood. Apocalyptic expectation conceived of its time in terms of specific moments in the future, and of its effects as cosmological. The character of God's revelation was held to be highly exclusive, so that few were to be associated with the radically new Zion that was to come. On the other

---

21. For usages during the same general period, see Rev. 11:15; 12:10 (cf. 1:9); 2 Pet. 1:11. The turn of phrase seems to have influenced the Gospel of John as well, where Jesus refers to "my kingdom" (18:36).

hand, traditions of Wisdom could see the kingdom as something a sage might come to know by means of patient reflection (see chapter 3).

Jesus was neither an apocalyptist nor an educated product of a school of Wisdom. He was a child of folk Judaism, a local rabbi who conceived of God's activity in terms of the social world he saw around him. He saw God active in that world, and his vision gave him an assurance of the future. In that his vision included a hope for the future, it was irreducibly eschatological. The kingdom was in the seed and in the growing, and awaited an all-embracing culmination (see pp. 91-94). There was indeed (to invoke a long-established convention) a "now" and a "not yet" implicit in his conception of the kingdom.

The kingdom for Jesus was also a palpable force, which expelled demons, healed, cleansed lepers, and raised from death, all the while announcing itself (Matt. 12:28; Luke 11:20 [see pp. 67-70]; and Matt. 11:5; Luke 7:22 [see pp. 112-113]). Its effects were as forceful as the love that the king's character demanded, and Jesus' formulation of that standard became emblematic of his position (Matt. 22:34-40; Mark 12:28-34, cf. Luke 10:25-37; pp. 105-106). His fellowship with many in Israel who were regarded as unclean was also a hallmark of his movement, because he held that their willing response to the kingdom made them pure (see Matt. 11:19; Luke 7:34; pp. 80-90). Finally, the Temple in Jerusalem was for him, as it was for the book of Zechariah (ch. 14 in particular), a place where all people were to join in festal worship (Matt. 21:12-16; Mark 11:15-18; Luke 19:45-48; John 2:13-22; see pp. 90-94, 115-126).

The activity of God that was Jesus' vision caught him in the field of energy between the poles defined by the "now" of his perception and the "not yet" of his hope. That temporal dynamism is intrinsic to his position. A cognate energy arced across the fields of the other dimensions. To see signs of the kingdom in a healed few carries with it a passionate longing for the restoration of the unhealed many. Love, once conceived, yearns for love enacted. To discover purity in forgiveness makes forgiving into a vocation. A Temple for the kingdom must be accessible for all, as approachable as a humble meal with friends.

The fit between the kingdom and Jesus' ministry was striking from the outset because the essence of Jesus' program was to enact and perform that vision of the kingdom that was his own. His vision was comparable to the understandings of contemporary teachers, and yet distinctive. Much modern discussion would portray Jesus as simply an apocalyptist or simply a symbolist in the tradition of Wisdom. Either alternative makes Jesus easier to assess because he can thus be classified with categories of thought that are well documented. But the texture of early Judaism was more varied in its language of the kingdom than such reductive categories will allow, and Jesus was the center of a movement because he was a creative teacher.

Jesus' new model kingdom was more dynamic than most because he emphasized its identification as God's own activity, and he called those who heard him to enter into the tension between what God was doing and what God was about to accomplish. By the time the Synoptic tradition emerged, Jesus' movement was indeed a primitive form of Christianity: Jesus had been identified as the center of divine revelation, so that the kingdom was identified completely with him. That the kingdom is heralded, advocated, and guaranteed by Jesus is important first of all because that is the seal of his purpose, not because the kingdom is at issue in itself (see pp. 134-138 above).

The subsequent development of the New Testament confirms the tendency of the Synoptics. Indeed, we might see the logical outcome of the identification of Jesus and the kingdom in Origen's remark that Jesus was the kingdom itself.[22] The transformation of the center of the movement from the kingdom to the Christ was predicated on two conditions. The first was that the kingdom of God could be misunderstood as politically seditious within the Roman Empire; focus on a person made the pacific aims of the Church clearer from the outset. The second was the growing confidence that the story of Jesus as presented in the Gospels constituted an account of divine action that was more accessible and more credible than parables of the kingdom such as Jesus himself had told.

Neither of the conditions of the transformation of the kingdom into the Christ obtains in public discussion today. The pluralism of political ideologies that has long characterized the modern world permits the kingdom to be considered in its implications for policy. Those who are attracted to Jesus' preaching, whether they identify themselves as Christian or not, need not be reserved in their passion to suit what we do as a people to what God would make of us. And the experiential

22. Karl Ludwig Schmidt cites Origen's dictum (in his commentary on Matthew, 14.7) approvingly, although he takes the term *autobasileia* in a direction of his own; cf. "E. The Word Group βασιλεύς κτλ. in the NT," and "F. Βασιλεία (τοῦ θεοῦ) in the Early Church," *Theological Dictionary of the New Testament* I, ed. G. Kittel, tr. G. W. Bromiley (Grand Rapids: Eerdmans, 1978) 576-593, here 589, 593.

imagery of the parables may strike many today as more credible than the elaborate, largely secondary developments that the Gospels represent. Jesus' gospel of the kingdom may claim a hearing on religious grounds within its own terms of reference, quite aside from whether the bulk of the interpretations in the New Testament are accepted.

Among those who stand within the tradition of the Church's various orthodoxies, of course, the claims of the kingdom are also of moment. The person whose message was the kingdom was God's only son. Even if the most important aspect of faith is his status in relation to God, we may identify him within human terms of reference better by what he says than by any other indication. He who taught a distinctive vision of the kingdom and disputed its meaning with others is that person who was raised from the dead; apart from a knowledge of his message, we know not who was raised.

The new model kingdom, then, may not be overlooked, whether one's perspective is that of a general interest in religion or of orthodoxy in a Christian sense. Perhaps this is a good time to acknowledge that Jesus' vision was of a divine activity that was under way, forceful, loving and demanding love, embracing God's people in the purity of forgiveness, and reaching out from Jerusalem to include all. In the wake of the long Cold War, a hundred forms of parochialism claim the banner of Christianity and proceed to "cleanse" the earth of their ancient enemies in the name of freedom. Before our peace turns more violent than the static confrontation that preceded it, a new model kingdom may offer a hope of peace in the name of the Gospels.

"He comes to us as One unknown, without a name, as of old, by the lake-side, He came to those men who knew Him not."[23] Schweitzer's closing paragraph is often quoted, but as we have seen in the first chapter, it was only Jesus as a spiritual force who had continuing interest for Schweitzer. Jesus' spiritual heroism, Schweitzer wrote, resided in his commitment to the eschatological illusion that the kingdom would arrive while he was on the cross. And in the moment of his death, which was the failure of eschatology, the living example of his moral commitment was born. Schweitzer embraced that formulation of what he called "negative theology."[24]

---

23. A. Schweitzer, *The Quest of the Historical Jesus,* tr. W. Montgomery (London: Black, 1910) 401.

24. Schweitzer, *The Quest of the Historical Jesus,* 396.

Nearly a century after Schweitzer first published his study, we understand Jesus' theology much more clearly as a Judaic theology. Jesus' conception of the kingdom was of God's own activity, the divine performance of power, which could also be performed in human words and deeds. The obsession with eschatology that has hampered discussion can now be resolved. The tension between what God now does and what he will do on the final day is simply part of the quality of how God reveals himself. The time we live in indeed does not live up to the expectations of the time of the kingdom, just as the space we live in, the actions we perform, the objects we touch, and the people we reach out to are not to be identified with the kingdom. Jesus' decision to speak in parables (as we have seen in chapter 4) and to act in parables (as we have seen in chapter 5) reflected his clear awareness that the kingdom was a dawning reality, not a completed result.

The dawn of God's rule was a critical moment for Jesus. The problem was not that the issue of eschatology was more difficult than the issues of transcendence, ethics, and purity. Those coordinates of the kingdom were commonly recognized. The crisis for Jesus was rather that the kingdom that he preached and enacted, in performances that he had his disciples copy, was by definition a more public matter than many of his contemporaries maintained. Because he claimed it was not esoteric but accessible to perception and action, the question had to be pressed (pp. 90-97): from what point is the kingdom extending itself in its radiant power?

Jesus' occupation of the Temple and his final meals with his followers were his answer to that question, and answering it cost him his life (pp. 115-126). His vision of God as king was complete, because he performed it in all its five dimensions. The vision was complete, even as the kingdom itself was incomplete, continuing its dynamic realization among those who shared Jesus' vision. His vision generated meanings among the disciples then as it does now. (They had to confront, for example, as Jesus did not, the divisive question whether those outside Israel might be included in the celebratory meals of the kingdom.) Those meanings can be studied, understood, arranged in their order of generation, simply enjoyed. And they may also be enacted. He who was once unknown is now much better defined than it was fashionable a few years ago to think was possible. The vital question today is less his identity than our own.

The Divine King
in the Book of Psalms

The history of the emergence of the book of Psalms is complex, but four types of attitude toward the Temple have been detected. Because the Temple is the focal concern of the collection, four stages in the development of the book may also thereby be distinguished. Those stages correspond, in their turn, to four kinds of reference to God as king.

In the first stage, cultic assertions associated with worship even before the establishment of the Temple, some in connection with other gods, were brought into the sphere of the LORD's worship in Jerusalem. Although stage one is of foundational importance, it may be known only inferentially. Stage two is accordingly the point of departure here, the stage at which settled sacrifice in Jerusalem is the assumed setting. The destruction of the first Temple in 587 BCE provided the setting of stage three, which reflects a desire for the rebuilding of the Temple and the punishment of Israel's enemies. The fourth and last stage is the most explicitly eschatological. It envisages the inclusion of the nations in worship on Mount Zion within the context of a cosmological renewal that will make the Temple there a new reality.

The present appendix is designed to discuss the relevant passages within their stages so that the historical unfolding of the dimensions of meaning of the divine kingship might be appreciated. Those dimensions have been brought together in chapter 3, so that the convention of speaking of God as king might be appreciated as a whole.

Stage II

The statement toward the close of Psalm 22, "for the sovereignty is the Lord's and he rules among the nations" (v. 29, according to the numbering of the Hebrew text, as throughout this appendix) may appear to be a claim of sovereignty that is so general that it is theoretical. But within its context the assertion provides a specific locus for the claim that God rules as a king. The term "sovereignty" (מלוכה) is indeed more abstract than the more usual "kingdom" (מלכות), but it is equally rooted in the conception of divine kingship. The reason it is used here instead of the more usual term has to do precisely with the range of the rule that is claimed, among the nations, not merely over or by means of Israel.

The reference occurs at the close of a psalm that itself requires little rehearsal: the speaker has moved from a position of complaint (vv. 2-19), through one of appeal (vv. 20-22),[1] into the praise of God (in view of his response to the humble supplicant) before the congregation, which includes those who fear the Lord, the seed of Jacob (vv. 23-25).[2] V. 26 proceeds with the praise of God in the great congregation and a promise to fulfill vows before all who fear God. The act in view is a type of sacrifice of sharings: consumption by the poor, those who seek God, is an occasion of their praise (v. 27).

The "sacrifice of sharings" (*zebaḥ shelamim*, Lev. 3:1)[3] was an

---

1. The precise wording of the end of v. 22, "thou hast answered me" (עניתני), suggests that the appeal has been heard, which eases the transition to the next phase of the psalm. The wording of the beginning of the appeal picks up that of the complaint in v. 12, while v. 22 echoes vv. 13, 14.

2. It is conceivable, but no more than that, that the seed of Jacob is to be taken as additional to those who fear the Lord in v. 24. The sense would then be that all those who worship God, as well as Israelites, are to join in the recognition of the divine response. But the reference to the seed of Jacob in v. 24b is followed by a call to the seed of Israel in v. 24c: it seems plain that those who fear the Lord, the seed of Jacob, and the seed of Israel all refer to the same congregation. For that reason, the present section of the psalm is provided with an antecedent in the first section's rehearsal of what the holy one, enthroned on the praises of Israel, did for "our fathers" (vv. 5, 6).

3. Baruch A. Levine (*In the Presence of the LORD: A Study of Cult and Some Cultic Terms in Ancient Israel* [Studies in Judaism in Late Antiquity; Leiden: Brill, 1974] 3-52) caps his discussion with a description of the שלמן as "an efficacious gift of greeting," but his argument has been trenchantly refuted by Gary A. Anderson (*Sacrifices and Offerings in Ancient Israel: Studies in their Social and Political Importance* [Harvard

institution that the Priestly source attempted to routinize. The notion that a sacrifice might involve worshipers in a meal is a commonplace in ethnographic studies, and it is specifically attested in patriarchal and Mosaic narratives.[4] Jacob formalizes his treaty with Laban on that basis (Gen. 31:51-54), and Jethro celebrates both the LORD's greatness and the presence of Aaron and the elders thereby (Exod. 18:9-12). In 1 Sam. 1:3-5, that Elkanah should distribute sacrificial portions in his own household is recounted as a matter of course. In the Priestly source, however, burnt sacrifice and cereal sacrifice gained in importance at the expense of the sacrifice of sharings. But that demotion could not obscure the enduring place of the *zebah shelamim* within the tradition. At the time of the sacrifice to solemnize the covenant, Moses, Aaron, Nadab, Abihu, and the seventy elders are particularly said to behold God, eat, and drink, and that festive communion is most naturally associated with the *zebahim shelamim* referred to in the text (Exod. 24:4-11). The association obtains in royal provision for feasts together with sacrifices, whether the king involved be David (2 Sam. 6:17-19), Solomon (1 Kgs. 3:15; 8:62-65), or Hezekiah (2 Chron. 30:22). The Priestly source had to regulate a form of sacrifice that had a life of its own within the community (and before its community). Psalm 22 demonstrates the inclusive range that might be claimed as appropriate for the sacrifice of sharings.

The body of Psalm 22 is to be assigned to the pre-Exilic period, when "the theology of the Psalms was chiefly a theology of the Temple."[5] That is

---

Semitic Monographs 41; Atlanta: Scholars, 1987] 36-55). However one adjudicates that scholarly dispute, there is a consistency of stress on the co-participation (that is, co-consumption) by worshipers in the rite that the notion of gift does not convey, and Levine himself emphasizes the status of the sacrifice as a communal meal (pp. 26, 38, 41). Even in a text from Ugarit that Levine cites (p. 10, *UT* 611), the king partakes (ילחם) of the שלמן. If the sense of gift is defensible etymologically, "peace" and "well-being" cannot be excluded. All three senses may be understood as operative, provided the fact of sharing is noted. As Anderson correctly concludes, the sacrifice is "best defined as a festive meal" (pp. 51-53; cf. also Martin Noth, *Leviticus: A Commentary*, tr. J. E. Anderson [London: SCM, 1965] 31).

4. For a fuller discussion, cf. B. Chilton, *The Temple of Jesus: His Sacrificial Program within a Cultural History of Sacrifice* (University Park: Pennsylvania State University, 1992) 45-67.

5. Hermann Spieckermann, *Heilsgegenwart. Eine Theologie der Psalmen* (Forschungen zur Religion und Literatur des Alten und Neuen Testaments 148; Göttingen: Vandenhoeck und Ruprecht, 1989) 252.

the settled, generative period of psalmic ideology, when the songs of cult comported with the sacrificial activity that constituted the heart of worship.

At just the stage of the sacrifice of sharings, however, the psalm takes a turn and widens the horizon of participation in praise beyond even the "great congregation" of v. 26. "All the ends of the earth," "all the tribes of the nations," it is said in v. 28, are to take cognizance of the LORD, return to him, and worship before him. That is the precise context in which it is asserted in v. 29 that global sovereignty is the LORD's: the psalm envisages a situation in which God's support of the supplicant, now obviously understood to be Israel, draws the nations into sacrificial worship. They, "all the fat of the earth," are to eat and worship before him (v. 30a),[6] and the psalm closes with an assurance that the people so joined to God will acknowledge him (vv. 30b-32).

God's sovereignty, the simple recognition of his rule, is portrayed in Psalm 22 as appropriate to the nations, not only Israel, to the extent that those joined in that recognition might even take part with Israel in sacrifice. By differing means, the psalm voices the inclusive vision of Israel that animates Zechariah 14.[7] That development of a radically inclusive eschatological perspective (22:28-29, perhaps v. 30) attests the extent to which, as Spieckermann suggests,[8] the cultic stage of the Psalm served as a foundation for later developments.

Although the reference to the kingdom in Psalm 22 reflects later developments, the body of the psalm manifests a confident assertion of the value of cultic sacrifice in Jerusalem that is redolent of the period of the monarchy. Another such psalm, attributed to David, is Psalm 5. That psalm presents an appeal to God as king within a supplication (v. 3); the psalmist is distinguished from those who are evil, boastful, deceitful, or violent in his readiness to enter the Temple and worship within the fear of God (v. 8, cf. vv. 5-7). The paradigmatic importance of entry into the Temple in Jerusalem is a hallmark of developments at

---

6. That is the clear meaning of the Masoretic Text, which is correctly rendered in the King James Version.

7. Indeed, there may be an allusion to Ps. 22:28 in Rev. 1:7, which is a mixed citation of Daniel and Zechariah (especially 12:10) that finishes with the prediction that "all the tribes of the earth will mourn over him." It has been suggested that Gen. 12:3 and 28:14 lie behind "all the tribes of the earth," but the sense of those passages seems distant from that of Rev. 1:7, while כל משפחות גוים in Ps. 22:28 comports well with the wording as well as with the meaning.

8. Spieckermann, *Heilsgegenwart*, 252.

stage two. That is the standard, within Israel here, of those who trust in the LORD and receive his blessing and protection as righteous (vv. 9, 12, 13). The psalmist speaks for all those who pray and offer sacrifice,[9] then to await a divine response (v. 4). Psalm 5 establishes incidentally that the language of divine kingship might be applied exclusively within Israel to contrast the righteous and the wicked.

The similar headings of Psalms 5 and 22, sacrificial songs attributed to David, are consonant with their setting in stage two in our scheme. Psalm 93 proceeds without attribution or initial notation, appearing in a discrete section of the entire work that is entitled "book four" (the heading before Psalm 90). The first book consisted principally of psalms of David (1–41), the second principally of psalms of David, the sons of Korah, and Asaph (42–72),[10] while the third mentions Asaph principally, with the sons of Korah and David also in prominent positions (73–89).[11] The fourth book (90–106) and the fifth book (107–150) are the most eclectic. Some psalms are attributed to biblical figures, and some evidence a conscious reflection on biblical themes; others are unattributed and/or are placed in straightforwardly liturgical settings (such as the Sabbath, pilgrimages of the ascent of Zion, and lamentation); others still take an ascription to David as the occasion to explore issues of theodicy in a personal key, while overt complaints tend to be anonymous.

Leopold Sabourin represents the point of view that proper names prefixed by ל were "probably understood at first as a *lamed of attribution* or of *classification*, not of author," so that they represent the sort of composition or the usage of a psalm, rather than its authorship.[12] Sabourin himself discerns three earlier collections, "Yahwistic" (3–41), "Elohistic" (42–89, with a "Yahwistic supplement" [!] in 84–89), and "Later Yahwistic" (90–150).[13] He cites alternative hypotheses, and stresses that the dating and the collection of the psalms have been

---

9. The term ערך refers to the setting out of sacrifice. Cf. Leopold Sabourin, *The Psalms: Their Origin and Meaning* (New York: Alba, 1974) 218-220.

10. The "book" closes with an ascription to Solomon at the head of Psalm 72.

11. As in the case of the second book, the third ends with a psalm that presents a new heading, Ethan the Ezraite in the case of Psalm 89.

12. Sabourin, *The Psalms,* 14, 15.

13. Sabourin, p. 9. See the comparable scheme of A. A. Anderson, *The Book of Psalms* (New Century Bible Commentary; London: Oliphants, 1972) 25-27. Generally speaking, Anderson pursues a conservative agenda, contenting himself with references to more critical opinions. His views will be noted here only when they are exceptional.

matters of deep and widespread disageement.[14] It therefore seems wise not to suppose that any single scheme of chronology is correct, but (as here) to infer the setting of a psalm from its meaning and to accord secondary characteristics (such as attribution, heading, musical rubric, and inclusion in a given "book") only a supporting role in the inference.

Psalm 93 itself praises God as regnant and refers to his royal splendor (v. 1a, b)[15] in the same breath as his establishment of the earth (v. 1c). The three themes of divine rule, the echoing of appropriate praise, and the ordering of creation in such praise are coordinated in vv. 2-4 as well. V. 5, however, is the true climax; Jeremias argues (pp. 26-28, 39) that it attests confidence in the Temple, such as characterized the period of the monarchy, and he sees in vv. 3, 4 reminiscences of Canaanite myths of struggle with chaos (pp. 21f.). He emphasizes (p. 17) that the psalm concerns the enduring efficacy of divine rule, not its acquisition. Janowski's criticism of Jeremias is convincing insofar as Jeremias's attempt to sustain the argument in purely grammatical terms (as the nominalizing of a Canaanite myth) is concerned, but Jeremias's thematic insights appear valid, as Janowski largely grants.[16] The purpose of the psalm is to harness the cosmological pretensions of cultic worship as the peculiar attribute of the LORD. The Temple is here the locus where the primordial

---

14. Sabourin, *The Psalms,* 6-24.

15. The imagery has been taken to suggest that Psalm 93 and similar psalms reflect a festival of divine enthronement. That such a feast was celebrated in Israel is entirely possible, although the support for the hypothesis is as slender as the interpretation of the annual enthronement of Marduk (the analogy often alleged) is complicated. The hypothesis has recently been defended by Bernd Janowski (pp. 404, 413), in the context of his criticism of Jörg Jeremias (pp. 398-418). (Janowski's article is "Das Königtum Gottes in den Psalmen. Bemerkungen zu einem neuen Gesamtentwurf," *Zeitschrift für Theologie und Kirche* 86 [1989] 389-454; Jeremias's book is *Das Königtum Gottes in den Psalmen. Israels Begegnung mit dem kanaanäischen Mythos in den Jahwe-König-Psalmen* [FRLANT 141; Göttingen: Vandenhoeck und Ruprecht, 1987].) Even Janowski, in the course of discussing the hypothesis, redefines its import by referring to the representation of the divinely royal power by means of images of the royal God's rise to power (pp. 424-446).

16. From the work of E. Otto, Janowski picks up the emphatic claim that "JHWH ist Herr über das Chaos, weil er die Königsgott ist" (pp. 406, 408), rather than a deity that acquires its title as a result of victory over other gods. Janowski compares the psalm to Egyptian hymns to Re as triumphal god of the sun (pp. 409-412); constant ascendancy over chaos is therefore celebrated.

establishment of the world is appropriated as a presently experienced event.[17] The LORD's testimonies — his regulations within that Temple[18] — are said to be sure, and holiness is identified as the property of his house (v. 5): that is, the witness of the Torah and the conduct of the Temple are linked directly to God's cosmological rule. Obedience[19] and worship in Zion are the human analogues of the thundering rivers that declare the divine majesty (v. 3).

Stage I

The close association between God's rule as king and his chosen people in their land is evident in Psalm 24. His creation of the earth and what fills it implies that the range of his sovereignty is without limit (vv. 1, 2), but the center of his rule is Mount Zion, his holy place (v. 3). The principal issue of the psalm is the purity required to ascend to that place (v. 3), which is said to involve innocence in deed and integrity of heart, such that one neither desires what is vain nor swears deceitfully (v. 4). Those who so seek God (v. 6) are rewarded with blessing and righteousness (v. 5). The idiom of the psalm shifts to a welcome of the entrance of the king of glory, pictured as victorious in battle (vv. 7-10). The entrance of the divine king may be thought of as from the east, with the light of the sun at the autumnal equinox,[20] or — as seems more likely[21] — from his sanctuary, for a meeting with his chosen people in their act of sacrifice. Jeremias (pp. 62f.) argues that the emphasis of the psalm falls on the LORD taking Zion

17. So Janowski, "Das Königtum Gottes in den Psalmen," 418.

18. Janowski, 415 n. 94; for further reflections on the sense of the verse within a pre-Exilic psalm, cf. Sabourin, *The Psalms,* 199-201.

19. The emphasis on obedience may explain the survival of the psalm; it could be sung even with the Temple in ruins. But the formulation itself is not a simple product of the rational theodicy of the Deuteronomistic movement.

20. For a recent defense of the hypothesis, see Robert J. Daly, *Christian Sacrifice: The Judaeo-Christian Background before Origen* (Studies in Christian Antiquity; Washington: Catholic University, 1978) 52-61. Sabourin, *The Psalms,* 407-409, is more cautious.

21. After all, "everlasting doors" are to be lifted up, in order to permit the king of glory to enter (vv. 7, 9): God is to meet his people by proceeding from the very center of his creation. See Anderson, *Sacrifices and Offerings,* 205.

into his own possession, so that the cultic importance of the site previous to its association with יהוה is taken for granted.[22] Similarly, Spieckermann fastens on the epithet "the king of glory" as of Canaanite origin (p. 223); the LORD — and no other — is on his reading identified as the king of glory in vv. 7-10. But whether Psalm 24 is seen as an ancient and repeatable celebration of divine power or as a reminiscence of the coup that put Zion under the LORD's control, the psalm clearly relates the themes of the universal reach of the divine rule exerted from Jerusalem, the purity demanded by God, and his meeting with Israel in the role of conqueror. Psalm 24 is clearly closely related to Psalm 93, but it seems to belong more to stage one than to stage two because the emphasis is more on the identity of the god in the Temple than on the continuing efficacy of the Temple.

The setting of Psalm 29 is at first explicitly heavenly: the sons of gods are commanded to ascribe glory and strength to the LORD (vv. 1, 2). Much as the reach of divine rule in Psalm 24 is held to be without limit, although centered on Mount Zion, so in Psalm 29 the heavenly locus of the divine rule is fully consistent with its cosmological dimension, and "glory" is the connecting link (cf. vv. 1c, 2a, 3b, 9b). God's thundering voice is held to shudder through creation (vv. 3-9a) from its origin over the waters (v. 3a, c). Those waters are also the "flood"[23] over which God is enthroned (v. 10a), installed as king forever (v. 10b). The heavenly and cosmological rule of God, however, is associated particularly with the worship of the LORD on Mount Zion: "in his Temple all his[24] say 'glory'" (v. 9c). That assertion comes, as if incidentally, in the midst of overtly cosmological and heavenly imagery. Indeed, so casual is the reference that one might conclude that the temple at issue is the heavenly court rather than the Temple in Jerusalem. Jeremias in fact conceives of the base of the Psalm (in vv. 3, 9, 10) as the transfer to the LORD of Canaanite traditions.[25] But then, in v. 11, comes the promise that God will give strength to his people and bless them; worship in the Temple is held to produce prosperity (as in the book of

---

22. Jeremias therefore opposes the exegesis of the psalm that sees an annual festival of enthronement as its matrix.

23. For a brief discussion of the difficulty of rendering למבול (which cannot detain us here), cf. Janowski, "Das Königtum Gottes in den Psalmen," 420, 421.

24. The sense is that all those who serve God join in the cry.

25. Jeremias, *Das Königtum Gottes in den Psalmen,* 29-45, so also Spieckermann, *Heilsgegenwart,* 221; Janowski, "Das Königtum Gottes in den Psalmen," 418.

Deuteronomy).[26] The pattern, then, becomes clear: the heavenly attribution of strength to God (v. 1) corresponds to that worship in the Temple (v. 9c) in which God is pleased to give strength and peace to his people (v. 11). Spieckermann (p. 221) describes Psalm 29 as the exemplar of its motivating concern: the return to the LORD of glory in the form of praise in order to confirm and effect the reception of his glory. God is king precisely as such heavenly and cosmological themes are linked to the promise to his people. The association of the heavenly and earthly sanctuaries is particularly developed here in the interests of the LORD, and the attribution of the psalm to David (as in Psalm 24) suggests that the underlying ideology of stage one has been articulated in the context of the second stage. Indeed, the distinction between Psalm 29 at stage one and Psalm 93 at stage two is notional: their continuity is the more striking feature.[27]

Psalm 48 is the last representative from stage one, and it is assigned to the sons of Korah (cf. 42, 44, 45, 46, 47, 48, and 49). As with psalms attributed to David (especially 22 and 24), those attributed to the sons of Korah articulate an understanding of God's rule in which its epicenter is the Temple and the tendency of its range is without limit. In both collections it is perhaps more accurate to characterize the conception as radically inclusive than as universal. God is not conceived of as equally revealed as king over all the nations of the earth, nor is there any hint of a rationalistic theodicy to the effect that what is fully given to Israel is at least partially evident in what other peoples have seen of God. The implicit claim is rather that all who recognize the revelation of God on Mount Zion — but they alone — may enjoy his exaltation as king over all the earth.

The LORD is said in Ps. 48:2 to be great and to be well praised in

26. When his people keep the commandments, that ensures that the LORD will give possession of the land to them, thrust out their enemies, and — above all — give them physical and agricultural prosperity and freedom from disease (Deut. 6:17-19; 7:1-16; cf. also 4:32-40; 8:1-10; 11:8-17). The motif of prolonging days in the land is another Deuteronomic idiom of prosperity (4:40; 5:16, 33; 6:2, 3). For a linguistic discussion see Moshe Weinfeld, *Deuteronomy and the Deuteronomic School* (Oxford: Clarendon, 1972) 345.

27. Indeed, it is useful to keep in mind Janowski's caution, against Jeremias's acceptance of an appropriation in the north of a Canaanite conception of divine monarchy, that the motif of the LORD's kingship may have been a development within the worship of the Temple in Jerusalem ("Das Königtum Gottes in den Psalmen," 422-424).

"the city of our God, his holy mountain." That center, then named afresh as Zion, is said to be the joy of all the earth, the city of the great king (48:3). The place and the promise of Zion is defined by the juxtaposition of God's faithfulness in the midst of the Temple with his praise to the ends of the earth (vv. 10, 11). The reference in v. 3 to Mount Zion as in "the furthest part of the north" (ירכתי צפון) may constitute an indication that the psalm was produced in an environment in which Judah was understood as the ordinary geographical limit of the people of Israel. Mitchell Dahood takes the phrase as "the heart of Zaphon," that is, as a reference to Mount Casius, which featured centrally in Canaanite religion.[28] On that understanding, Zion is presented here as the navel of the universe, a construction that suits the present reading. Although the Ugaritic parallels illuminate the origin of the phrase, its geographical meaning must have been dominant after 721 BCE.[29] Spieckermann (p. 288) cites Psalm 48 as of the essence of the theology of Psalms generally: praise of the saving presence of the LORD as king in his sanctuary (cf. pp. 222-223).

Stage III

By way of both confirmation of and contrast with our reading of Psalm 22, the usage of Ps. 10:16 (also a supplication) may be observed. There, the issue is also vindication, in the shape of the punishment of the wicked and the establishment of the poor (cf. vv. 15, 17, 18). The imagery is personal, in its reference to social conditions and intentions (vv. 2-11, 13), and yet abstract in its lack of specification, as God is asked, in conformity to his own nature, to reverse injustice (vv. 12, 14, cf. v. 1). V. 16 breaks in on the development of that plea with a claim of divine sovereignty that effectively identifies those outside Israel with the wicked:

---

28. *Psalms I* (Anchor Bible 16; Garden City: Doubleday, 1966) 288-290. Further support, and reference to Isa. 14:13, 14, is provided by Hans-Joachim Kraus, *Psalmen* I (Biblischer Kommentar Altes Testament; Neukirchen: Neukirchener, 1960) 343.

29. Sabourin, *The Psalms,* 208-209, holds that the phrase "heart of Zaphon" is "archaizing," and stresses the importance of geography for an understanding of the psalm, which he places at the end of the sixth century.

> The LORD is king forever and ever,
> the nations shall perish from his land.

The language of royal rule is naturally invoked in the psalm, and
— once it is invoked — the association with complete triumph over the
enemies of Israel is a regular feature of the received understanding of
God's kingship. The original association of Psalm 10 with Psalm 9, with
which it shares a single acrostic structure,[30] confirms the impression
that the language of individual lament is applied here to national disaster. The psalm is comparable to Psalm 74 in its transfer of the rhetoric
of individual complaint to the people in their defeat.[31] The address of
theodicy in the experience of exile, an ancient theology in the midst of
nearly genocidal destruction, is the hallmark of stage three.

In the psalms said to be "of Korah," the notion of God as king
takes on an apparently personal dimension. In Ps. 44:5a, the psalmist
breaks in with the claim that God is his king. The personal acclamation
of God follows a rehearsal of how God won the land for "our fathers"
in vv. 1-4. What appears to be personal, then, is essentially paradigmatic:
immediately after the acclamation comes the appeal, "Command the
victories of Jacob" (v. 5b). The psalmist identifies himself as a particular
instance of a warrior in Israel in that he realizes that his weapons no
more assure triumph than those of his predecessors (cf. vv. 7 and 4).
From v. 10, the communal condition is described as one of defeat and
exile, and the psalm culminates in an appeal for help (vv. 24-27). The
imperative in v. 5b should be taken as proleptic of that appeal: a paradigmatic warrior is appealing to his king for aid,[32] and the foundation
of the appeal is maintenance of the covenant (v. 18). The covenantal
promise in the midst of national calamity is a hallmark of stage three.

Psalm 74 is attributed to Asaph and presupposes the destruction
of the Temple, perhaps even the vilification of an Antiochus (cf. vv. 1-11,

---

30. Cf. Sabourin, *The Psalms*, 279-282. But he fails here to follow his own criterion
(p. 192) that later psalms incline toward the form, an indication of relative lateness that
Anderson, *Sacrifices and Offerings*, 105-106, acknowledges.

31. Cf. Spieckermann, *Heilsgegenwart*, 159.

32. By comparison, the Septuagint (43:5) is prosaic at this point. "My king" and
"my God" are used interchangeably, as titles, and a participle represents the imperative.
The effect is to make a global and abstract assertion of divine power and to obscure the
link between the halves of the psalm that the conception of divine kingship helps to
achieve.

18, 21-23).[33] The reference to God as "my king from of old" here is by way of reference to his saving acts on behalf of Israel "in the midst of the earth" (v. 12), including his acquisition of Zion for his dwelling (v. 2c). The rehearsal of those acts together with the ordering of creation in vv. 13-17 is reminiscent of the song of Moses and the Israelites in Exod. 15:1-18 (cf. vv. 16-18 in particular). Psalm 74 is a classic example of stage three, comparable to Psalm 10 (as the opening of both psalms would suggest). The specific reference in 74:20 — in a manner consistent with the usage in 44:18b — to the covenant, as the ground on which God should act, is another link with the theology of the exodus, and the reminiscence of "victories" in v. 12 comports with the usage of 44:5b. In comparison with earlier psalms, Psalm 74 assumes a tighter identity between Israel's fortunes and God's rule as king in that his failure to act royally in the context of so much destruction is held to call his covenant into question (v. 20).

Spieckermann argues that Exod. 15:1-18 is the earliest extant psalm with a *"heilsgeschichtlichem Sujet,"* namely the exodus itself and the possession of the land. He links the text of 15:18 to the acclamation of Baal as king in a cultic context (pp. 157 and 110), and such a context is consistent with the express reference to the sanctuary (15:17) immediately prior to the royal acclamation (cf. also vv. 11, 13). Spieckermann goes on to suggest that, although the *"heilsgeschichtliche Überlieferung"* might have been known within the worship in the Temple, it was not used intensively until the existence of the Temple became problematic, as in Psalm 74 (cf. pp. 158-160). He argues that Exodus 15 represents a survival from the domestication of Canaanite myth (p. 157), which is probably a correct assessment of its ultimate provenance. But it is perhaps more straightforward to see in its focus on God's kingship in his sanctuary a reflection of the generative concerns of the exile, such as occasioned the redaction of the sources known generally as the Yahwist and the Elohist. Jeremias (p. 100) similarly analyzes Exodus 15 as a newly interpreted myth of Baal, but he strongly opposes the analysis of Cross and Freedman, according to which the song antedates the national period (p. 105). The *heilsgeschichtlich* taming of the myth is for Jeremias evident here in a way that it is not elsewhere (in Psalm 93, for example, also on p. 105). Our judgment is closer to Jeremias's than to Spiecker-

---

33. Even Sabourin, *The Psalms,* 301-304, who is generally skeptical of a Maccabean hypothesis for the generation of psalms, inclines toward that identification.

mann's and is supported by the use in Exod. 15:17 of "Lord" (אדוני) as a replacement for the tetragrammaton (יהוה), which seems to be an indication of later psalmic usage (cf. 44:24 and 22:31). In any case, Spieckermann's citation of Ps. 74:2 as an allusion to Exodus 15 (p. 113) is apposite and underscores the deliberate echoing of earlier themes in Psalm 74, which we have seen is characteristic.

Psalm 95 manifests a similar interest in the *Heilsgeschichte* of Israel (cf. vv. 8-11), and functions transitionally for Psalm 96 (which, as we shall see, represents stage four). Jeremias associates Psalm 95 with the period between the first and second deportations, in that the continued efficacy of the cult appears to be presupposed (p. 113), but the interest at stage three in the explanation of catastrophe in terms of a rational theodicy is evident: a "hardening of heart" has afflicted Israel, as it did once at Meribah (v. 8; cf. Exod. 17:1-7; Num. 20:1-13, 24; 27:13, 14; Deut. 32:51; 33:8). The rock to which one sings (v. 1) is he who brought forth water from the rock, and destruction is the consequence of rebellion against him.

God's dominions, taken as plural (ממשלותיו in Ps. 114:2b, cf. ממשלתו in 103:22), are understood in Psalm 114 to refer to the Lord's (cf. אדון in v. 7) acquisition of Israel from Egypt. The interest in locality is marked by the statement in v. 2a that Judah was God's sanctuary, in parallelism to the assertion that Israel constituted his dominions. That shift to a more local, but still celebratory, emphasis, is consistent with "book five" of the Psalms generally (cf. the ascription prior to Psalm 107). In aggregate, they constitute songs of national deliverance; the festive purpose of the Hallel (Psalms 113–118) for celebrations involving pilgrimage is particularly marked. Nonetheless, the language of rule is used here in the context of cosmological imagery: the retreat of the sea at the exodus and of the Jordan for Joshua (vv. 3, 5), the quaking of the mountains (vv. 4, 6), all before the God of Jacob (v. 7), who provided water from the rock (v. 8). Those events assert his dominion, and they establish Israel as his dominions, Judah as his sanctuary: God's activity as king is again linked closely with the fortunes of his people. The celebration of saving acts, associated with the exodus, as an assurance of God's presence among his people, is emblematic of stage three (cf. Spieckermann, pp. 159-160), as the reference to God as "Lord" (cf. Exod. 15:17; Ps. 44:24) and the incident of drawing water from the rock (cf. Ps. 95:8) would also suggest.

The final reference to God as king in the book of Psalms, at Ps.

149:2b, appears in the doxological conclusion of the book (Psalms 146–150), and illustrates the persistent tendency of the language of divine sovereignty to focus on Zion and on the joy of the chosen people (vv. 2-6), the "poor" (v. 4b), at the expense of the nations (vv. 7-9a). The imagery combines festal celebration by means of dance and music (v. 3), even singing on couches (v. 5b), with the use of swords and fetters in order to execute vengeance on the nations (vv. 6b-8). The language represents a desire for recompense following a fearsome decimation.

Stage IV

The apparently personal dimension of the kingdom in the psalms of the sons of Korah is perhaps better considered paradigmatic (cf. Psalm 5), as our reading of Psalm 44 would suggest. That possibility is confirmed in Psalm 47, where all the peoples are to acclaim that the LORD is "great king over all the earth" (vv. 1-3). But as in Psalms 22 and 29, although the horizon of the claim of divine sovereignty may be without limit, its focus is particular: his acquisition, at the expense of those peoples who are to praise him (47:4), of an inheritance *for Jacob* is the occasion of a renewed acclamation of LORD with shouting and the sound of the horn (47:5, 6). The site of the musical recognition of God as "our king" (v. 7) is evidently the Temple. There the people of Jacob can acclaim him king over all the earth (v. 8), specifying both that he rules over the nations (v. 9a) and that he is installed on his holy throne (v. 9b), Mount Zion itself. Those truly of the "nations" (cf. v. 9a) are in the position of awed impotence (vv. 3, 4): the implicit promise is that the currently reduced fortunes of Jacob are to be the occasion of global kingship, as the divine king whose inheritance is Jacob is recognized over all the earth (vv. 3, 5, cf. vv. 7, 8, 9). Psalm 47 ends with an emphatic assertion of the preference of Israel (v. 10):

> The nobles of the peoples are gathered,
> the people of the God of Abraham;
> for the shields of the earth are God's.
> He is highly exalted.

Those of Israel are in aggregate the nobles of a larger group, those peoples (העמים) as a whole who are called in v. 2 to acclaim God in submission to Jacob (cf. vv. 4, 5). The full vindication of Jacob's inheritance is an inalienable aspect of the revelation of God's kingdom, even within a claim of its extension without limit. Precisely because he is the God of Abraham (v. 10), an inherent privilege attaches to any assertion of his rule. Nonetheless, the hallmark of stage four is the radical inclusion of the righteous among the nations within that rule.

The range of God's rule according to Psalm 96 is as wide as is usually claimed at stage three, but the extent of God's rule is taken as the occasion to stress that his majesty is to be made known among those outside Israel. The whole earth is called to sing a new song to the LORD, to recount his glory and his wonderful deeds among the nations (96:1-3). The next phrase, "For great is the LORD and greatly to be praised" (v. 4), is an echo of Ps. 48:2, and the psalmic theology of Zion is also taken up here. The LORD's status as the creator of the heavens is stressed at the expense of the gods of the peoples (v. 5; cf. 97:7), so that majesty and splendor are before him (in heaven) and strength and beauty are in his sanctuary (v. 6). The "tribes of the peoples" (v. 7; cf. 22:28) are on that basis commanded to acknowledge the LORD by bringing offerings to his Temple: all the earth is to writhe before him (vv. 7-9). The next phase of the Psalm (beginning with v. 10, as cited here) is particularly telling for an understanding of the divine kingdom on the basis of the book of Psalms generally:

> Say among the nations that the LORD reigns.
> The world is established, so as not to move:
> he shall judge the peoples with equity.

God's kingship is cosmological and is expressed in v. 10b by means of the same wording that appears in 93:1c; here, however, it is also linked to an eschatological judgment of everyone on the earth. The final verse (v. 13) emphasizes that aspect unmistakably, after an intervening reference (in vv. 11, 12) to the joy of the entire creation:

> before the LORD, for he comes,
> he comes to judge the earth,
> he will judge the world with righteousness,
> and the peoples with his truth.

160

In addition to the old Psalmic theologies of Zion and of God's cosmological rule, an eschatological emphasis is apparent within Psalm 96 that relates the universal claim of God's rule to the universal judgment that is to come. The local aspect of the sanctuary in Zion is not treated as in the least inconsistent with the eschatological emphasis. On the contrary, the sanctuary's strength and beauty reflect the divine majesty and splendor (v. 6): Zion is precisely the point at which God's sovereignty is recognized and the focus from which the divine sovereignty will radiate. The eschatological emphasis is characteristic of stage four, as the derivative language of v. 7 (cf. 22:29) and v. 4 (cf. 48:2) suggests.

The assertion that the LORD reigns in Psalm 97 (v. 1) celebrates his sovereignty in principally cosmological terms (vv. 2-6, 9), but the theology of Zion remains emphatic (cf. v. 8), however vital the theme of universal recognition has become (cf. vv. 5b, 6b, 7). Such a twofold emphasis is characteristic of stage four. Those two aspects are united in a single insistence on the righteousness that derives from God (vv. 2b, 6a, 8c) and that God sustains (vv. 10-12). His justice is what makes God accessible and evident to all, which is why those who join in his holy worship are — of necessity and by definition — the righteous (v. 12).

Psalm 98 also takes up familiar themes and repeats the imperative to sing a new song to the LORD (v. 1a; cf. 96:1a; 33:3a; 40:4a; 144:9a; 149:1a) in view of his coming as the universal and final judge of the peoples (v. 9, cf. 96:13). The latter motif is the most prominent indication that the psalm is best understood as constituting a unit with Psalm 96. The psalm portrays God's actions in respect of Israel as exemplary: what he has done for them, particularly in gaining victory for them, is held to warrant universal and cosmological recognition (vv. 1b-8). It is striking that such recognition is assumed to be consistent with the call to celebrate the divine glory with the musical instruments of the Temple (cf. vv. 5, 6a). The language of God's kingship is prominently deployed precisely as the language of the cult is also introduced (v. 6b).

That pattern is manifest in the next psalm as well. The motif of royal sovereignty is the instrument of insisting that the LORD is enthroned both in a cosmological sense (99:1, 2b) *and* in Zion (vv. 2a, 4c, 5f., 9) in such a way as to command recognition by all peoples (vv. 1a, 2b, 3), and especially worship by those like Moses, Aaron, the priests, and Samuel for the judgment and righteousness wrought by God in Jacob (vv. 4-7). V. 1 shows how the cosmological theme is a vehicle for the expression of radical inclusion. Moreover, the ancient motif of the divine king's assurance of the stability of the earth (cf. 93:1c) is now swallowed up in the eschatological prospect of dissolution. Jeremias takes 99:6f. as an emblem of a Deuteronomistic, exilic theology. In her fuller study, Ruth Scoralick has concluded that a priestly understanding of the psalm as an exilic rereading of the threefold praise of God as holy in Isaiah 6 is more plausible.[34]

The juxtaposition between cosmological and local enthronement characterizes usages that might be mistaken as simply universal — Ps. 103:19, for example. The references to the establishment of God's throne in the heavens and to his kingdom as exercising dominion over all may appear — taken out of context — simply to celebrate a kingship that is available and accessible generally. But the psalm is a summons in the by now familiar form of a paradigmatic first person (addressing himself) blessing God (vv. 1, 2) for his forgiveness, healing, redemption, provision, and restoration (vv. 3-6) as made known to Moses and the sons of Israel (v. 7). That disclosure is the locus within which God's fatherly care is evident (vv. 8-16). Immediately prior to v. 19, an assertion of the LORD's חסד for those who fear him, keep his covenant, and remember his prescriptions (vv. 17, 18) provides the immediate context within which it is sensible to declare the sovereignty of the LORD in v. 19. The next three verses represent the same qualification: the messengers of God who perform his command are summoned to bless him (v. 20), together with the heavenly host that does his pleasure (v. 21) and all his creatures who recognize his dominion (v. 22a, b): within that setting, the summons of the soul of the paradigmatic psalmist (v. 22c, cf. v. 1a) receives its meaning. The heritage of stage three here is evident in the emphasis on a single sphere of worship, heavenly and earthly, defined by the Mosaic covenant; its reality transcends the Temple, and therefore also its destruction. But the radically inclusive extension of that reality to "all" (v. 19, cf. vv. 6, 13, 17) is a hallmark of stage four.

Psalm 145 appears in a larger section of book five of psalms attributed to David (from the heading of Psalm 138). In most of them, the principal issue is deliverance, either as sought or celebrated, and the implicit setting is generally worship in the Temple, and Psalm 145 is agreed by Sabourin to be "one of the latest in the Psalter." The figure of

---

34. Ruth Scoralick, *Trishagion und Gottesherrschaft. Psalm 99 als Neuinterpretation von Tora und Propheten* (Stuttgarter Bibelstudien 138; Stuttgart: Katholisches Bibelwerk, 1989).

David may be taken as paradigmatic of faithful Israel, and v. 3 has him take up the refrain that the LORD is great and greatly to be praised (cf. 48:2; 96:4) as part of an exaltation of the divine king (v. 1). The references to the kingdom in vv. 11-13 are embedded precisely in that model of paradigmatic praise: v. 10 speaks of *all* his creatures giving thanks to the LORD, but it is his faithful in particular who are said to bless him (v. 10b). They speak of the glory of his kingdom and his might (v. 11), making them known to the sons of man (v. 12), in that his kingdom and dominion are eternal (v. 13). The divine rule extends to every place and creature, especially as he supports those who are fallen or distressed and nourishes every living thing (cf. vv. 14-16): the LORD is righteous and faithful in all (v. 17, cf. vv. 7, 9), near and responsive to all those who call on him (vv. 18-20a), even as he will annihilate the wicked (v. 20b). The last theme may appear unexpected until it is recalled that some of the divine imagery at the beginning of the psalm may be taken as martial (cf. vv. 4b, 6a). The final image in v. 21, that all flesh should bless the holy name of the LORD, is inferentially an ideal realized for the moment only in the place of his holiness.

Implicitly, then, a setting in the Temple is presupposed in Psalm 145, and that link between God's universal rule and Zion — as is consistent in stage four — becomes explicit in the next psalm. There, paradigmatic usage of the first person singular conveys a general imperative to praise the LORD (146:1, 2) in which his power is recognized as above any human dominion (vv. 3, 4) and as universal in the scope of its support, very much as in Psalm 145 (vv. 6-9). But allegiance to the LORD, the God of Jacob, is the condition of blessing (146:5). The particular privilege of those who are oppressed, whether by physical or social conditions, is marked (vv. 7-9); God loves the righteousness (v. 8c) and subverts the way of the wicked (v. 9c). The final statement, that the LORD will reign for ever, is doubled with the identification of him as the God of Zion (v. 10). The Temple is the center of a rule that is without limit and that is to be recognized as such, but the authority of that rule is a righteousness that is necessarily exclusive of the wicked.

Jesus' Prayer and
the War of Worlds

Jesus' most famous prayer has long been caught in a tug of war between popular devotion and critical scholarship. For the most part, popular devotion has held the day in churches, while universities have provided a reasonably skid-free terrain for scholarship.

The devotional perspective offers what seems a straightforward interpretation of the petition "lead us not into temptation, but deliver us from evil." We are taught that we ask God here to keep us from wicked impulses; the battleground is a heart we seek to keep pure. As English has developed, "temptation" has come increasingly to refer to "entice-ment" (to use the diction of *The Oxford English Dictionary*). The result has been that some people seriously imagine that Jesus' prayer involves the rejection of human passion in itself.

The scholarly view has it that the petition refers to the final, apoc-alyptic judgment of the world. The point, we are told, is that we ask to be spared in the ultimate conflagration. Rev. 3:10 promises that those who keep Jesus' word will be guarded from "temptation" (*peirasmos* in Greek, *temtatio* in Latin), and in context the reference is clearly to apocalyptic trial. The scholarly interpretation has been taken up in some sectarian groups and pressed for the assurance that members of the sect concerned will be physically removed from the earth at the end of all things.

It is easier to refute both positions than to establish either. The term "temptation," reflecting the Latin *temtatio* (with variations of spelling), is intended to refer to a trial or test, not some personal failing. (Cicero even uses the word to refer to attacks of disease.) And the evil we seek rescue from is best translated "the evil one," the devil. The devotional interpretation, with its general request to ward off bad things, appears imprecise and slack. On the other hand, the phrase "deliver us from evil" appears only in Matthew's version of the prayer (6:13; compare Luke 11:4). Within Matthew, the phrase plainly refers to escaping the devil's wrath (as in 13:19, 38); English translations obscure the point, but Matthew's phrase in Greek *(ho ponēros)* refers more to evil as personified ("the evil one") than to evil in the abstract. Before the usage is taken as a guide to Jesus' meaning, however, we need to recall that the entire phrase, "Deliver us from the evil one," is probably an expansion. As in the case of the clause concerning God's will, the Matthean version explains what could be a difficult concept to understand. Just as "Thy will be done" explains "Thy kingdom come," so "Deliver us from the evil one" explains "Lead us not into temptation." So although critical scholarship has been right in insisting that the meaning of the phrase is apocalyptic, its own findings show that it is Matthew's meaning, not Jesus', which is at issue.

What has happened is that popular devotion has invented a new meaning out of "temptation" *(temtatio)*, which in Greek *(peirasmos)* and Aramaic *(nisyona)* refers to testing or trial. But Matthew and scholarship have also invented a fresh meaning, which imposes a rigid view of final judgment on Jesus.

Commentators have been inclined to seek some compromise between the two views. Their hedging is reflected in available translations, which commonly soften the Greek text of Matthew, so that it appears to refer to the avoidance of anything tempting and evil in general. Marginal notes sometimes try to take back the apocalyptic sense of Matthew that the translation itself has given away. False compromise is usually a bad way to solve a problem, and the present case is no exception to that rule. What is needed instead is an understanding of the position of Jesus that generated the two interpretations we have mentioned (and others).

Jesus simply prayed, "do not bring me to the test," or in Aramaic, *'al ta'eleyni lenisyona.* Although there was a biblical tradition of the testing of heroes of faith, such as Abraham (see Gen. 22:1), it was also acknowledged that trials could be directed against such antagonists as

Egypt (see Deut. 4:34; 7:19). Jesus' position was that, in calling God our parent, we ask him never to put us to the ultimate test, which might prove us unworthy. It is neither a plea against our own impulses nor a request to be spared an apocalyptic conflict, but the appeal of trusting children to remain with their father whatever might come.

Index of Names and Subjects

Index of Scripture
and Other Ancient Writings

Made in the USA
San Bernardino, CA
01 October 2013